# DESKTOP

*Dollars & Sense*

# PUBLISHING

## SCOTT R. ANDERSON

# DESKTOP
## *Dollars & Sense*
# PUBLISHING

## Scott R. Anderson

## Blue Heron Publishing, Inc.

# Desktop Publishing: Dollars & Sense

Copyright © 1992 Scott R. Anderson

Library of Congress Catalog Card Number 92-70718
ISBN: 0-926085-51-7

**Publisher's Cataloging-in-Publication Data**

Anderson, Scott R.
      Desktop publishing : dollars & sense /
   Scott R. Anderson. -- 1st ed. -- Hillsboro,
   Or. : Blue Heron Pub., c1992.

      p. ; cm.

      Includes index.
      ISBN 0-926085-51-7


      1. Desktop publishing--United States--
   Management.    2. Small business--United States
   --Management.            I. Title.

   Z286.D47A      070.59'068'0973 dc20
                                 92-70718

Cover graphics and design: Marcia Barrentine
Electronic publishing and inside design: Dennis Stovall

First Edition, First Printing
Printed in the United States of America on acid-free stock

Blue Heron Publishing, Inc.
24450 N.W. Hansen Road
Hillsboro, Oregon 97125
503.621.3911

# CONTENTS

ACKNOWLEDGMENTS ................................................................ viii

INTRODUCTION ........................................................................ ix

CHAPTER 1    IN THE BEGINNING… .......................................... 1
It's a new day and you're the boss ....................................3
Decisions, decisions.............................................................4
Moving on .......................................................................... 13

CHAPTER 2    FINDING YOUR BUSINESS BASE ........................ 14
Defining your market niche .............................................. 15
The dreaded "M" word...................................................... 17
This little piggy went to market… ....................................28

CHAPTER 3    WHAT'S IN A NAME? ........................................ 30
The name game ..................................................................33
Getting it right the first time ............................................36
Tooting your own horn ......................................................36

CHAPTER 4    THE PRICE OF DOING BUSINESS ........................ 40
Beginner's syndrome ........................................................ 40
Setting your rates.............................................................. 44
Where has the time gone? ................................................ 45
Choosing time and expense software ............................ 48

CHAPTER 5   BACK TO BASICS ...................................................... 49
  Doing business with business ...............................50
  Dangers of growth ...........................................55
  Collecting on receivables....................................58
  Cash flow and marketing ...................................61
  Barters and trades .............................................61

CHAPTER 6   PENNIES IN YOUR POCKETS ............................ 63
  Picky clients and "profitless" customers ..........................63
  Some general guidelines ...................................72
  Walking the tightwire .........................................73

CHAPTER 7   ALL FACTORS CONSIDERED ............................... 74
  Oh where, oh where has all the cash gone? ...................76
  Offering terms — where credit is due ...............78
  A lending hand — maybe ...................................80

CHAPTER 8   DOING THINGS BY DESIGN ............................... 86
  The good, the bad and the ugly .........................87
  High-resolution vs. low: quality vs. quantity ...................91
  Sizing up your competitors ...............................95

CHAPTER 9   FOR YOUR PROTECTION ................................. 100
  Get it in writing................................................ 101
  Client responsibilities........................................ 103
  Protecting your business ................................. 107
  When to hire the legal beagles ........................ 108
  Rights and copyright........................................ 109
  Taxing situations ............................................. 111
  Choosing attorneys, CPAs
    and other professionals ............................... 112

CHAPTER 10  MINDING YOUR P'S AND Q'S:
            THE DANGERS OF LIBEL .................................. 115
  What is libel? ................................................... 116
  The cost of libel .............................................. 118
  A political tool? ............................................... 119
  Your best protection ....................................... 119
  Defending against libel ................................... 122
  Insuring against libel....................................... 125
  Mind your own business — invasion of privacy ........... 130
  Defenses against invasion of privacy............... 134

CHAPTER 11  MINDING MORE P's AND Q's:
 COPYRIGHTS & WRONGS ................................ 135
Who owns the copyright, and for how long .................. 136
Do your homework ........................................ 139
Hide and seek, copyright style ......................... 142
Other red flags ........................................ 145
Beyond copyright ....................................... 149
Registering your copyright ............................. 149

CHAPTER 12  CHOOSING THE RIGHT TOOLS ....................... 151
Basic choices .......................................... 152
Recommendations ........................................ 154
When to upgrade ........................................ 158
Typesetting vs. DTP..................................... 161
Choosing a service bureau .............................. 161
Tools of the future ................................... 164

CHAPTER 13  ADDING DOLLARS THROUGH DIVERSITY ..... 166
Making the best choices ................................ 168
Narrowing the selection ................................ 171

CHAPTER 14  FINDING THE LOOPHOLES ........................ 174
Legitimate loopholes ................................... 174
Questionable practices ................................. 178
Business ethics........................................ 178
Illegal practices...................................... 179
Keeping secrets ....................................... 180

CHAPTER 15  WHERE TO GO FROM HERE ........................ 182

INDEX ................................................... 187

# ACKNOWLEDGMENTS

A book of this nature is not possible through the efforts of just one person. Special thanks are due to attorneys Bob Hughes, Marshall Nelson, Frederic M. Wilf and Dan Riviera, without whose help the chapters regarding legal matters would not have been possible; to publishers Dennis and Linny Stovall for their incredible patience throughout this project; and to Jane Scarano of *Cut & Paste* for all of her assistance and encouragement.

Others who have contributed immensely to this book, whether their names are mentioned elsewhere or not, include Marguerite Ellen, Ron Wodaski, Carol Pentleton, Jim Dornbos, David Cole, Jeanne MacGregor, Heidi Waldmann, David Boe, Judi Wunderlich, Stephanie Hopkinson, Dale Hart, Lora Burgoon, Andy White, J. Michael Marriner, Brenda Garno, Barbara Dill, Larry Worrall, C.J. Metschke, Chad Milton, Paul and Sarah Edwards, Vaugh Misail and the National Association of Desktop Publishers, and Theresa M. Coady.

My apologies to those who may have been interviewed for this book and who are not mentioned here. It's not a sign that you're contribution isn't appreciated, only a reflection on the sometimes helter skelter state of my desk over the past several months of interviewing, making notes and trying to keep up with other business matters.

# INTRODUCTION

W hen the idea for this book first started whirling in the back of my head in mid-1989, it was little more than a concept formed because, though I had several years of business experience as a publisher, I needed ideas for my then-new desktop publishing business. As time went on, I saw a continuing need among other desktop publishers for the same type of information I was seeking. Through a fortuitous set of circumstances, I won unlimited access to CompuServe's desktop publishing forum for a period of several days and the research I was able to do during that time further bolstered my confidence that the time was ripe for a book like this.

I first became acquainted with Dennis Stovall through a series of phone calls on matters completely unrelated to this book. I met Dennis in person while attending the Pacific Northwest Writers Conference in July of 1991 where I casually mentioned my interest in writing a book about desktop publishing. Dennis didn't waste a beat in replying that he was looking for a book about desktop publishing.

Interestingly enough, this book almost never came about because initial research on Dennis' part showed a similar book already on the market. I purchased the book, read it with a critical eye, refined my outline and returned it to Dennis. He called back to give the project a "go," convinced that it was substantially different from the other book.

This book focuses on specific areas and problems likely to be faced by desktop publishers, writers, graphic artists and others whose businesses have evolved from the days of the traditional print shop to today's often home-based one- and two-person desktop publishing businesses. It's hoped that desktop publishers of all types will find useful information here, but the book is approached largely from the perspective of the home-based and small one- and two-person operations. It's impossible to know exactly how many desktop publishers there are, but a good guess would be at least several hundred thousand. The Seattle phone book lists well over a hundred; the Portland, Oregon, phone book, two hundred. Even locally, a dozen are listed; at least two others known to be in business do not have ads in the Yellow Pages.

At its least, desktop publishing is a set of editorial and creative design tools that allow us, for printing projects, to do in minutes complex tasks that once took hours of painstaking concentration. At its best, desktop publishing's much more than that, allowing us to wrap a hug and a kiss around every client's project as if we were sending our own child out the door to face the world on her own for the first time.

One of the hardest things about writing a book of this nature is selecting which information to include and which to leave out. Dozens of people graciously took hours of time to be interviewed for this book. I've tried to select the best quotes and most illustrative examples for the situation being discussed. Inevitably, this led to omitting good quotes and examples that were repetitious or which, finally, did not quite fit the needs of a chapter. Even those I interviewed but did not quote made a significant contribution, giving me a broader perspective on the scope of desktop publishing in North America.

For those who picked up this book expecting a "get-rich-quick" formula for success, I have bad news. Desktop publishing is not a "get-rich-quick" business. Yes, you can make a good living from it and yes, you might even get rich from it if you combine it with other revenue sources — and if you have a good head for business. But you're not going to do it with 20 hour weeks sitting on the sunny beaches of Hawaii or California, unless you're extremely lucky. Most desktop publishers reported working at least fifty- to sixty-hour weeks, and much of that time is spent on marketing. Without a marketing effort, it's difficult to find clients, and without clients it's hard to stay in business.

Many of us would like pat answers to dilemmas we face frequently in business: what marketing techniques work best, what doesn't work, what's the best way to set rates, how to deal with difficult clients. As we'll see, there are no pat answers to many of these questions, only broad guidelines that can give us a sense of where we're going and what to expect once there.

# CHAPTER 1

# IN THE BEGINNING...

Home-based or one- or two-person desktop publishing businesses, take heart. This book's for you. It's also for writers, editors, graphic artists, consultants and others wanting to build a more stable income base by offering additional services. Many who are already working in related fields will find the transition to desktop publishing logical, if not necessarily always easy.

As with any business, success in the desktop publishing field hinges on many variables. Even in today's "instant everything" society, business success isn't likely to come overnight. Just as for anyone in any business, desktop publishers need a sound grounding in basic business principles to build the best chance for success. Even with that knowledge, it's likely to take several years of hard work to get a business on firm financial footing.

It is possible to learn these fundamentals the hard way, "seat of the pants" through trial and error. I've done it. My publisher's done it. So have many others in the business world. So have many, many more who tried it and did not succeed. Personally, I don't recommend it. Especially with today's vast resources that, in some cases, are available at the touch of a key. Library shelves offer dozens of books on business basics, along with dozens of books about fundamentals of desktop publishing design, electronic composition, digital graphics, and all the other pieces of the puzzle. Electronic databases are packed with information that can help businesses of all types. Universities, community colleges, chambers of commerce and other local organizations offer a variety of courses geared to small business. Even the IRS schedules frequent workshops aimed at helping out the small business. And even the U.S. Postal Service provides regular seminars on effective business use of the mail.

Success in the desktop publishing field doesn't hinge solely on having solid business knowledge, though. If it did, we'd all be rich. Other influences include how well we identify with our clients and their needs; how thoroughly we understand typography, design, and the interaction between words and graphics; the effort we put into marketing; how we price our services, how well we do so and whether we adapt our pricing structure to ever-changing needs and technology; even, in some cases, how well we understand potential legal problems.

Another influence is attitude. Successful businesspeople I know don't look at their involvement in past businesses that didn't work out as "failures" but rather as learning experiences. It's like learning to walk. Most of us don't learn to do it on our first try. But as long as we keep trying, most of us eventually succeed. There is one big difference, of course. It doesn't take money to learn to walk. Sometimes, it doesn't take money to start a business, either, at least not much. But it does take money to keep the doors open for another day.

Whether you've already started your desktop publishing business or are only considering the step, this book is here to help you make the right business decisions. The reasons to start your own business, or expand an existing one from a related area into desktop publishing, are endless. You may already have a solid grounding in writing, editing, graphic arts, typesetting, printing or some related field — or you may simply be sorting out possible first career choices. No matter your starting point, desktop publishing has the potential of being a personally satisfying and financially rewarding occupation.

Let's set the stage for our discussion, though, by assuming we're all at the beginnings of self-employment together.

# It's a new day and you're the boss

You've always wanted to be your own boss but you've been afraid to take the plunge. Or maybe you feel you've never had enough money to strike out on your own.

There's no question that starting your own business can be risky, but there are ways to do so and reduce the risk. Each year, more than 600,000 new businesses are started in the United States, and most are small businesses. Within five years, however, the doors will close on more than 90 percent of these. Why? All else being equal, what makes one company succeed while a competing firm shuts its doors?

To most people, running a business seems easy. Almost daily I hear people claim they could run a business better than its current management. You hear it from co-workers, in line at the grocery and, perhaps most frequently, from employees of the small businesses that have become the backbone of America's economy. Running a business — even a small, home-based service business — is more complicated than it first appears, as the new businessperson soon learns.

At first, the demands can seem overwhelming, starting with the incredible amount of paperwork. Fortunately, computers have made coping with paperwork at least bearable. For the small business, moderately priced, basic financial programs offer even us non-accountants easy-to-learn double entry bookkeeping systems. Combined with the services of a good CPA, knowledgeable in your field, accounting jitters can be overcome in months. But the new businessperson daily faces a barrage of decisions, many of which will directly or indirectly affect how the business

operates, its profitability, the business' ability to acquire or upgrade its equipment, its credit policies, and so on.

# Decisions, decisions

Since business demands often seem overwhelming, it's easy to
overlook important issues. Things like

- the need to have at least a basic understanding of libel,
  copyright, and invasion of privacy, and the potential
  problems each creates for desktop publishers;
- factoring and other financing methods, along with how
  to effectively check credit and collect on past due accounts;
- attitudes toward design and setting fees, and which approach will work best for the market niche and public
  image you want for your business;
- pricing methods and how to operate profitably;
- types of marketing, and how to use them best; and
- how to plan the growth of your business.

The desktop publisher who caters to bargain-basement price
hunters and the DTPer who goes after only clients who want a
quality product both may have viable businesses, but each will
use entirely different methods to position him- or herself in the
marketplace.

The decision-making process should start well before business
doors open, and failure to do this, along with lack of capital, accounts for many business failures. In an interview for this book,
Paul and Sarah Edwards, authors of *Working from home: Everything you need to know about living and working under the same
roof,* repeatedly emphasized the need to thoroughly research a
business idea *before* startup.

Many, if not most, small businesses start up undercapitalized,
often because they neglect to research costs and, less often, because the businessperson realizes more capital is needed but takes
the risk anyway. Despite lack of capital, some succeed. At the

same time, starting with lots of capital does not guarantee success.

Certainly, chance can influence success — being in the right
place at the right time with the right service. More often than not,
however, those in the right place at the right time with the right
service have done their research, know the market and know
there's a demand for their service.

"While you still have a job," say the Edwards, "take time to
research and plan for your business. Find out exactly what other
people's experience has been and the amount of time it takes
them to succeed and what works with customers," for instance,
"if it's a business that flourishes with advertising, whether it be
Yellow Pages or in publications. Go to back issues of Yellow
Pages, see how the ads change, if the companies stick around or
if they're there from year to year.

"Do your homework in every possible way that you can so
that when you get into business you have a realistic idea of how
much money it's going to take, how to get business, what to
charge, what people will pay for. All that information is like an
investment that you draw upon and adds to your success.

"The first and most important thing is, if you have a job, hang
onto it. Start your business part-time using cash flow from your
employment to finance your startup business and test it out.
Don't jump into a cold shower, giving up your job and finding
out whether or not you can warm the shower water by virtue of
your enterprise and whether your idea works and whether you're
suitable for being your own boss. Start small, start part time."

It also pays to use some discretion in starting a part-time business, even if it's home-based. Progressive employers often encourage employees with entrepreneurial leanings to try their wings
and often your employer can be one of your first clients. Other
employers, however, view dimly any part-time enterprise, seeing
it as competition or as a lack of total commitment on your part
to the company. You'll want to find out which type of employer
you have. After all, you don't want to end up with no income to
finance your venture before you even begin.

In starting a part-time venture, it also pays to use a little common sense. If you work for a newspaper, for example, your employer will not be thrilled to learn that you're using your wages to start a competing publication or to offer related services and you're likely to find yourself pounding the pavement — or fighting tooth and nail to make your new venture succeed. At the same time, your chance of success is best if you stick with something you know, even if it's just a hobby. If you're a writer whose hobby is music, your chances of succeeding are far better if you buy or start a music store than if you go into the plumbing business and you don't know the difference between a pipe wrench and a plumber's helper.

## Sticking with it

Assuming you've found a suitable part-time enterprise, you've received a nod of encouragement from your employer and you're able to finance it through your job or with other resources, how long do you stick with it if it isn't succeeding? That, say the Edwards', is a difficult question to answer. "We find the people who've been successful don't achieve instant success, they go through hard times, it's difficult, and persistence becomes the number one quality. Over and over and over again we hear that successful home businesses have demonstrated that, more so than brains and more so than creativity, it's raw persistence," balancing that at some point with the desire to operate the business and reception in the marketplace.

## Working from home

One of the surest ways to reduce risk appears to be by operating a home-based business. On a trip to Pittsburgh, the Edwards' learned of a study that found that 97 percent of home businesses started there were still in business twelve months later — a phenomenal number, they say, though there is no way of getting information on businesses that don't file for licenses.

"The fact is that most home businesses don't get city business licenses and it may very well be that those people who took the time to know, to find out that they needed a city business license and went to the effort, were businesses that were more apt to survive than businesses that were started on the fly."

Though operating from home can mean additional expenses, say for a business telephone line and fax, it can substantially reduce overhead, eliminating additional office rent and utilities expense.

Care should be used in selecting a home-based business, however, because not all businesses are suitable for home-based operations and local ordinances may prevent operating certain types of businesses, or even any business, from home. In our community, for example, a home occupation permit is required if clients will be coming by the house, even infrequently, and no retail uses are allowed nor are funeral parlors. Some occupations, such as my wife's housecleaning business, are exempt from the permit requirement since only accounting and record-keeping for the business is done in the home but we still must have city and state business licenses and pay all appropriate taxes.

Licensing and permit standards vary from state to state and community to community, so the only way to find out is to check locally with the appropriate governmental agencies.

Operating from home is not an excuse for a lackadaisical approach to business; if anything, it requires attentive monitoring of cash flow and procedures and recognition of the need to separate personal and business finances. And while overhead can be kept lower working from home, operating a home-based business still requires capital. You must do your homework before beginning, particularly if you plan on pursuing your business full time. What will it cost? How much savings will you need, or how much must you borrow? Seldom is a new venture profitable enough to support you from the outset.

## Getting to know you

In any business, personal contact is vital to survival and home-based businesses are no different. "Home is your base, not a permanent place," Paul Edwards notes, "so you've got to get out and meet people, make contacts." Equally as important is building the solid, long-term relationships on which a sound business will ultimately rest — and prosper. This is a process that cannot be hurried, though it should be undertaken as soon as possible, and even before the business formally opens. Relationships are built on mutual trust, which takes time to develop. Certainly, making sales and generating income quickly are important to the health of the business and to your self-confidence, but your future demands the longer view, the construction of a base of customer relations.

When we start talking about building relationships, we begin to focus on marketing. But we're not talking here about mass marketing as done by the experts, with all its glitz and hype, but of marketing in the sense of letting others know about your services and how those services can benefit them.

I live in what many would consider a small city, with a population of 53,100 and a county population (including Bellingham) of 132,200. I have lived and worked in much smaller cities and communities and, for a while, I lived in Seattle, Washington's largest city. Building relationships works in communities of any size and, as long as you treat people fairly, the way you would want them to treat you, it's never going to hurt business. But the shear size of larger cities makes it more difficult to establish personal relationships with potential clients, so other marketing approaches are sometimes useful. Because of this, it should be obvious that the same marketing strategy will not work in every situation, yet I am constantly amazed at the number of businesses that open a branch locally or send sales representatives here that don't take this into account.

Putting aside, for a moment, the issue of building relationships, let's look at a more basic example. In Seattle, it's common to see men wearing business suits. A salesman dressed in a suit would feel at ease. Here in Bellingham, the business atmosphere tends to be more relaxed and, as a result, dress more casual. The salesman, while perhaps feeling a bit overdressed, still could feel comfortable. But in the farming community of Lynden, eight miles north, a salesman in a suit not only would feel uncomfortable, he probably would find it difficult, if not impossible, to close a sale.

## Leaving your comfort zone

While building relationships and observing local custom helps build business, that's not all there is to marketing. Sooner or later, in a service-oriented business, it is necessary to leave your comfort zone and make cold calls. All the advertising in the world will do you no good if you're not willing to follow up by calling on people, often people you've never met or even talked with. Business consultants recommend turning cold calls into warm calls before making the initial contact.

One way to do this is to select your prospects by how likely they are to need your services. This "prequalification" can be done by simple research in phone books and business directories. Or it can be facilitated by direct contact through memberships in business groups, especially those most likely to have potential clients as members. Organizations and other networks will provide many useful leads.

Carefully targeted mailings are another way to warm prospects before you pick up the phone to call. But key to this approach is putting effort only into mailings that you actually can follow up with real contact, by phone or in person. Doing large mailings that get stale before you can take advantage of them — or using a shotgun approach — will only shoot your budget.

By turning cold calls into warm calls, you've already started developing relationships, but the process has just begun. Too often, people unaccustomed to sales give up just when they are on the verge of succeeding. As publisher of small weekly newspapers a few years back, I repeatedly heard figures thrown out at workshops and seminars that the average salesman must make six to ten calls on a client before making the first sale. Reasons are many, but the most obvious are that the client is checking the salesperson out for reliability, dependability, trustworthiness and the client wants to be sure that the product or service you offer is something they really need and that you can deliver that product or service as promised, when promised. But, most importantly, it takes that long to start building a relationship, and the client is more likely to buy once that relationship is established.

## Paying attention to your finances

So far, we've focused on pre-startup considerations and marketing, but there is another area that often gets new businesses in trouble, and that is failure to pay attention to finances, including development of a business plan, cash flow, and billing procedures and credit policies. Reasons for business closures within the first five years vary. They include lack of adequate capital and medical problems without adequate insurance. But failure to pay attention to the financial side of a business plays a significant role in many business closures.

As a newspaper publisher who served double duty as primary ad seller, I often called upon new businesses whose doors opened simply because the owner had always wanted to be in a particular business, say a gift shop. Usually, no market research had been done nor any thought given to whether the community could support still another store of its kind. As more and more gift shops opened, it was obvious that somebody would have to close. The same with hardware stores, the clothing stores and the service businesses. Though there were exceptions, I found that businesses that opened their doors without doing research also were the most likely to approach their business finances casually.

Regardless of your business size — even if you only gross a few thousand dollars a year — the first steps in dealing responsibly with your business finances should be to establish business checking and savings accounts apart from your personal finances and, concurrently, to develop a business plan. It never hurts to have a full-fledged business plan in writing and your banker may require it if you want a loan.

# Planning your business

A business plan needn't be complicated but should take a realistic look at current and projected income, expenses, cash flow projections and anticipated equipment expenditures. It also should project anticipated company growth, both in terms of sales volume and expansion to new locations. A business plan should not be cast in concrete, however. Things change. Sales rise or fall, equipment needs change with technological advances, sometimes due to technological advances new services become available and old ones obsolete. The innovative businesses, the ones most likely to survive, remain flexible and adapt to change.

A business plan need not cover internal company policies, such as billing procedures and credit policies, but both issues should be addressed, ideally before you hang out your shingle. If, as with many service-oriented businesses, your company will rely heavily on accounts receivable you may wish to find good accounts receivable software or, if you're keeping books manually, to develop a good billing system. In either case, you'll want to consider how often to bill and how to handle past due accounts — whether to try to collect them yourself, send them to collection or go to small claims court. Thought also should be given to credit policy. A loose credit policy makes it easier to do business with you but also means more bad debts; if your credit policy is too tight, you may find it difficult to attract clients. The policies you choose for both billing and credit will have a direct bearing on your cash flow.

# The importance of cash flow

With a business plan in hand and a firm grasp on marketing through personal contact and building relationships, it's time to concentrate on the area that creates havoc for many service businesses: cash flow. Cash flow means nothing more than the amount of money actually entering and leaving a business. It seems a simple concept, and maybe that's why it can cause a business so much grief, because the amount of money a business carries on its books does not equate, necessarily, with the amount of money actually entering and leaving a business.

Let's say, for example, that a desktop publisher has $15,000 in accounts receivable on its books for December, but of that $15,000 only $7,500 is collected in January, the month that it's billed. Meanwhile, the company must pay $8,000 in outstanding bills in January. The company has a negative cash flow for January of $500. It is quite possible for this same company to be profitable, however, as long as it doesn't reach the point where expenses continually exceed collectible income.

The goal, then, is to is to maintain a positive cash flow as much as possible. A continually positive cash flow is a much nicer problem to deal with than fluctuating or continuously negative cash flow. As Harlan D. Platt points out in his book *Why Companies Fail*, "Cash flow cycles are a business reality. They lead to trouble only when sales are highly seasonal or when annual cash flow is negative. With proper management, the cash-flow cycle is easily overcome even when sales follow a seasonal pattern; however, ...trouble awaits firms that mismanage the cash-flow cycle."

Most startup companies will be dealing with either fluctuating cash flow or continuously negative cash flow. A fluctuating cash flow usually is preferable to a continuously negative cash flow but, for startup companies, costs of buying or leasing equipment and setting up shop or office can create a continuously negative cash flow for long periods, sometimes for the first several years. This is among the reasons that if you have a job it's a good idea to keep it and start the business part time. You may find it necessary to subsidize the business for some time before it becomes profitable. It should be equally clear, however, that no business can afford to lose money forever. If, after a few years of operation, your business still consistently shows a negative cash flow it's probably time to take another look at it, both from a standpoint of management as well as realistically assessing whether there is actually a demand for your services. Then you can decide whether you wish to continue subsidizing the business or call it quits.

# Moving on

In a nutshell, we've surveyed in this chapter some of the real issues faced by small businesses of all types, from the perspective of ideal situations. The realities of operating a small business, however, often force us to operate under conditions less than the ideal. The balance of this book explores in depth — from a real life, hands-on perspective — issues important specifically to desktop publishers and those in related fields, such as writing and graphic arts. Practices and theory applicable to small business in general are touched on only briefly here and are addressed more thoroughly in a dozen or more already published books. Since today's technology seems to change hourly, technical problems are not addressed and equipment discussions, when necessary, have been kept as generic as possible.

# CHAPTER 2

# FINDING YOUR BUSINESS BASE

When Paul and Sarah Edwards began writing about home-based businesses in the early 1980s, working from home was largely a lifestyle question. Today, there are 22 million full- or part-time home-based businesses plus 5.5 million Americans who regularly work from home on a salaried basis. "Because of the headlines we read every day about corporate 'downsizing,'" says Paul, "the corporation is not the secure bastion of employment it used to be. Consequently, a lot of people are looking to become their own boss as a matter of necessity.

"The ability to be self-employed is a survival skill for the '90s. Today's reality is 'you're on your own.' Your family is a real family, not a company family." The Edwards cite affordability of technology as a third major reason that more Americans are shifting to working from home, noting that it's now possible to buy a powerful computer, laser printer, copier and fax for a combined price of under $2,500. Just a few years ago, the total price of comparable equipment easily would have been between $5,000 and $10,000 — or more.

In their book, *The Best Home Businesses for the 1990s,* the Edwards profile desktop publishing as one such enterprise. However, they're quick to point out the importance of having a good visual sense along with technical ability and a willingness to learn. "We find that the people who are most successful are the people who put their energy into the business, not only in marketing, but also into preparation and learning."

## Defining your market niche

Interview dozens of desktop publishers for a book, and you soon learn that the possibilities for unique market niches are about as endless as desktop publishers' imaginations. C.J. Metschke of The Monterey Press, Inc., Grayslake, Illinois, focuses on editorial and desktop publishing services but markets those services within a network of three other one-person businesses. The four-person group calls itself Ibis. Charlene Anderson-Shea says the main focus of her desktop publishing business in Honolulu, Hawaii, is problem-solving. Heidi Waldmann of Choice Words & Graphics, St. Paul, Minnesota, does a lot of work for nonprofit groups. "I am theologically trained in chaplaincy so I identify better with non-profit groups," she says. "Identifying one's niche is important. I speak the language of non-profits."

Carol Pentleton of Chepachet, Rhode Island, has a one-person shop that focuses on design, media placement and writing advertising copy. David Boe of San Diego uses desktop publishing in his business but considers himself a graphic designer with a background in publishing. In Ogdensburg, New York, Brenda Garno works full time for a company during the day "and pretty much full time for myself at night" as a writer and desktop publisher. Jeanne MacGregor, owner of LaserType in Bellingham, Washington, calls herself a generalist but prefers book projects. The list of market niches could go on for pages.

With the array of possibilities, a logical starting point for a desktop publisher seeking that first client is to decide which types of clients or which types of projects you prefer. If you prefer a range of projects and clients, you may wish to call yourself a generalist and market your services accordingly. On the other hand, if you have expertise in a specific area and you can adapt it to desktop publishing, you may want to capitalize on that. Defining a market niche needn't be limited to startup desktop publishing operations, though. Owners of established desktop publishing firms can find their businesses suddenly heading in a direction that they don't want to go, or that they never considered. If that happens, it's probably time to review your market niche.

Another logical way to begin defining a market niche is to look at your own interests. If you like working with horses, for example, or you're active in a local kennel club, a newsletter for horse owners or dog lovers is a logical starting point for building a business. You might even develop enough of a reputation through the newsletter that you could add additional income by offering consulting services. Maybe you collect fire trucks, banana peel stickers, or slugs. Newsletters are published on just about anything these days, but if whatever it is you collect doesn't already have a newsletter, you've just defined a market niche.

As with developing a business plan, defining a market niche needn't be time-consuming or expensive. A little time spent at your computer or with pencil and paper jotting down goals, personal and work interests, and the type of projects and people you like to work with will go a long way in defining your focus. Once you've done that, you may wish to review your decision occasionally, just as you'd review a business plan. How often you'll want to consider your market niche will depend on your needs and how you've structured your business. For some, once a week is desirable. For others, once a week would be too much and once a year might be better. For nearly all of us, review is good at least occasionally. Technology changes. The nation's economy changes. The world changes. The weather changes. We change. Death and taxes are inevitable, the old saying goes, but even taxes change. The last I heard, death hadn't changed, making it the one constant in an otherwise ever-changing world.

# The dreaded "M" word

Whether we find them through word of mouth, direct mail, advertising, networking, volunteer work or some other approach, all of us need paying clients. Some desktop publishers have clients immediately upon starting their businesses. Others must seek them. Some established desktop publishers report that they have a steady flow of repeat clients. Others see cyclical fluctuations in their business because their marketing efforts result in large jobs for clients but, when the work's finished, they must start selling their services all over again.

All of us, whether we're startup operations or established businesses, need repeat business and we need to constantly be looking for new clients. Book after book about small-business success points out that one of the biggest dangers facing a small business is the tendency to rely on just one or two major clients. In a one- or two-person business, it's especially easy to fall into this trap. A client brings you a major project and suddenly you're swamped for several months with more work than you can handle. Just as suddenly, when the project's finished, you find the wolf knocking at your door because you've been too busy to do any marketing.

Ah, there it is. That dreaded "M" word.

Mere mention of the word strikes fear in the hearts of some of us. We don't like it. If we were to make a list of the top 100 things we like to do, it probably would be number 100 — or it might not even make the list.

But marketing doesn't have to be a big, bad, ugly word. In fact, it shouldn't be.

Regardless of our market niche, one of the things a small desktop publishing operation should be able to emphasize when talking with potential clients is a level of personal service that's often lacking in today's mega-corporation world. This should be as true for the small type shops that offer desktop publishing services, and which may be corporations, as it is for those of us who are one- or two-person home-based businesses structured as sole proprietorships or partnerships.

For businesses of this size, there's really nothing magical about marketing. There are a variety of proven techniques that work — and a few that don't. A lot of marketing hype is not needed and in my experience its use often leaves a prospective customer skeptical. What potential clients look for instead are your willingness to establish a long-term business relationship, as discussed in chapter one, and your honest, fair assessment and presentation of the services you offer. Price, while important, often is secondary to your level of service and attention to detail. Incidentally, persistence pays; you may need to explain your services more than once to the same prospective client before seeing signs of interest. Businesspeople, especially, often use this initial show of indifference to screen out salespeople who aren't willing to come back a second, third or fourth time.

# A ringing illusion

While you can find exceptions in the business world to just about every practice, there are certain marketing techniques that do not work well and which especially do not work well if used by themselves. For example, the Edwards cite the "ringing telephone syndrome." This is the illusion that you're making a marketing effort because you're sending out a flyer, brochure or doing some advertising. Then you sit back and wait for the telephone to ring, saying to yourself, "I've done my marketing for the day."

No doubt there are desktop publishers somewhere who've found this technique works for them. For most of us, however, it will not. Cold calling can work if you're good at it. Most of us are not. And even for those who are, direct mail cold calling will be more successful if it's followed up with other marketing tools, such as a phone call.

An alternative approach to the ringing telephone syndrome is a technique familiar to most freelancers: marketing is a regularly scheduled part of each work day or week. The form this marketing of your business takes depends on the types of clients you hope to find. Your promotions may involve mailings, ads, phoning, or visiting prospects where they work. But it may help to think of your effort as if you were doing it for someone else — for some customer who has asked you to design marketing materials and test them.

No matter what natural talents you bring to your desktop publishing businesses, its success depends on how seriously you take marketing. The more you practice marketing, the more effective you will become. So, it's not just one brilliant promotion that pays off, but building on all previous efforts.

As the Edwards note, "what you want is to get to the point that your business is self-generating, so that the amount of time you put into marketing goes down. For a business to be self-generating, you must be getting repeat business and referral business."

Even with a self-generating business, though, it's always a good idea to do some marketing. Businesses lose clients for any number of reasons — a business closes its doors, new owners take over a business and decide they'd rather do business elsewhere, a major client goes bankrupt or dies, a longtime client's buddy has just started a business that competes with yours so he's now going to take his business there. These are just some of the things that happen. If you're relying on one or two major clients and suddenly you lose them for these or other reasons, chances are your business will be in trouble, too.

# Word of mouth

Most of the desktop publishers interviewed reported their best source for finding clients was word of mouth. If you're offering good service this is the best, and least expensive, advertising you'll get. However, there is one hitch: if the quality of your work isn't acceptable, or if someone has a grudge against you and has a lot of contacts in your community and didn't like some work you did for them, word of mouth also is the quickest way to kill your business. As for the latter situation, if you've done a lot of work for other clients before someone like this starts bad-mouthing you, you'll probably weather the storm. If, however, a client like this is among your first you could find it's an uphill battle to attract new clients.

Brenda Garno says her marketing is totally word of mouth in Ogdensburg, New York, population about 14,000. Her contacts have come, she says, through a friend who's an insurance broker who "knows everybody," through membership in New York state's largest car club, and as the result of a brochure she made about a friend's car.

# Networking

Networking in the 1990s can mean traditional networking such as participation in service clubs or local organizations such as your chamber of commerce. Or it can mean making nationwide and even worldwide contacts via electronic bulletin board services and databases. Or it can mean joining a bevy of clubs or organizations that you find of interest. No matter how you define it, for many of us networking is an excellent way to meet prospective clients.

Networking can be formal, through participation in networking clubs; moderately informal, through membership in a chamber of commerce or by participating in a local service club such as Kiwanis, Rotary, Lion's Club, Toastmasters, etc.; or informal, simply keeping in touch with friends and family and letting them know about your business and your services. Even involvement in church activities can provide some level of networking, though this isn't necessarily an avenue that's going to bring you a lot of clients.

One of the best places to start networking is with competitors. The experiences of businesspeople in general bears this out. If you're familiar and friendly with your competition, they will be more likely to send overflow business your way, and you will be able to enlist them when projects too large for you come along. Where trade organizations exist that attract other desktop publishers, such networking is easy, but elsewhere it's easy to visit or pick up the phone and chat. This sort of sharing generally benefits one and all. In any case, it's important that you know who your competitors are and what they're charging for similar services. That's part of the ongoing research that began before you went into business.

While networking with competitors can be important, it can be equally important to continue other kinds of networking. At the same time, do the amount of networking that feels comfortable. Not all of us are social butterflies who feel a need to have our fingers in every community pie. Nevertheless, just like writers, most desktop publishers enjoy being around people when we're not cubbyholed away somewhere frantically working to finish a project on deadline.

Heidi Waldmann is an avid advocate of networking. She knows a lot of people, is active on the Compuserve desktop publishing forum, "and somehow I got known as the PC person to a lot of Mac people. I teach as well, so I meet people that way. It's important to network.

"My colleagues who find it more difficult to talk to people have a much tougher time getting business. Focusing like I do on a niche, that gets to be known, too."

Carol Pentleton says her networking technique "basically is just getting out and about and talking to people. Some is through local arts organizations, some through professional organizations for advertising people, some through community organizations."

For David Boe, networking is "mainly just staying in touch by phone with several people with whom I enjoy working. The phone's a real powerful tool."

A slightly different type of networking has worked for Lora Burgoon of Fitzwilliam, New Hampshire. A desktop publisher for a consulting firm for a little more than three years, she's been on her own and working from home since late 1991. Former co-workers at the consulting firm where she worked have found new jobs "and they're calling on me to do work for them. I am not the best salesperson, so it's been mostly word of mouth and referrals. I banged on every business door in the area and got 'we've been using so and so and we're not going to change.'"

## Personal contact

Use of networking techniques will bring personal contact. So will keeping in touch regularly with friends and family members. So can direct mail and telephone, especially once you've established a business relationship with a client or prospective client.

## Direct Mail

Targeted direct mail can be an effective means of promoting your business, but it's generally effective only if it's followed up with telephone calls or other personal contact. Phone calls are more effective if you've "warmed up" your cold calls as suggested in chapter one. At the very least, know the name of the person with whom you want to talk and be sure that this person has the authority to make a decision. It's best to find this out before you do a mailing, since it can take some time to find this information.

Jane Scarano, founder of Data Search Publications and publisher of the desktop publishing marketing newsletter *Cut and Paste* has found direct mail effective. The company began with a targeted mailing just to health clubs in the New York City metropolitan area. The targeted mailing was followed up with phone calls and the health clubs "were very responsive. It was easy to get our first clients."

Waldmann also has found success with direct mail. "When I started, I did one direct mailing to about 250 people that were hand selected. I didn't know them. They were chosen based on the probability that they would need my services. I got about 50 responses from a return post card and came out with about eight to ten jobs and five to six ongoing clients. From those and ongoing jobs, there were enough referrals to start."

## Telephone

For someone who's good at telemarketing and pure cold calling, the telephone can be an invaluable tool. It also can be a tremendous time-saver for the rest of us, once we've established a sound business relationship with a client. Once a relationship has been established, the phone provides some measure of personal contact, though often not as good as a face-to-face meeting.

When working with clients long distance, phone and fax are a necessity in today's business world, and the ability to send and receive faxes can be a tremendous convenience even on a local level, shaving minutes or even hours of otherwise wasted travel time off of a work day. Nevertheless, as a newspaper publisher it didn't take me long to realize that there are business people who do not like conducting business by phone. If you want them as clients, you see them in person.

It can take a few months of regularly working with clients to find out which are comfortable dealing with you by phone and which prefer personal contact. I place such information in my database and my tickler files for ready reference. With new clients who are local, if we start transacting business by phone and I sense some reluctance, I visit them. Often, they're simply uncomfortable working by phone.

Usually, as time goes on and clients get to know you better, they'll start easing up and things will go smoother. However, I have had clients who never became comfortable with working via telephone.

# Yellow Pages advertising

Yellow Pages advertising draws mixed reviews from desktop publishers. DTPers in the Chicago area report the cost of Yellow Pages advertising there is prohibitive for a small business. Others say they've found Yellow Pages advertising ineffective for their businesses. Still others say they get responses, but only from people who want bargain basement prices. In my area, Yellow Pages advertising is affordable so far and I get a reasonable number of calls. Many are the bargain basement price hunters but I also get occasional serious calls. And, it's one means of serving notice to anyone who wishes to check that we are a legitimate business.

# Giving out free information, writing articles

"Giving out free information establishes you as an authority," say the Edwards, and that can lead to business. So can writing articles about subjects that you know well or that you can convince an editor that you can research. In either case, you need to know where to draw the line so that you don't end up giving away the store and leaving clients with no reason to do business with you.

Consultants in any field earn top dollar these days and even in a recession they're not going to tell you everything they know for free. Good consultants, on the other hand, will tell you enough that you should be able to easily determine whether they know what they're talking about.

As for writing, not all desktop publishers are good writers and not all writers are good at desktop publishing. If you're fortunate enough to be good at both, this also can be a way to establish yourself as an authority. There may be occasional times when it pays to write an article gratis. In most cases, however, I strongly recommend that writers insist on reimbursement for their work. Many things need to be considered when looking at whether to allow free publication of an article, most importantly the kind and amount of exposure it will mean for your business, what the market for the article might be elsewhere (is there another paying market, for example), and the article's resale potential. In many cases, if a publisher is unwilling to pay for an article you can negotiate for an in-kind service, such as advertising space — after all, even cash payment is a trade.

If at all possible, however, get payment for what you write. Things are tough enough for writers today without having to compete against freebie articles. Desktop publishers who write also should be aware of various rights that can be sold or granted with an article. For detailed information, see the latest edition of *Writer's Market*, available from bookstores or from Writer's Digest Books.

# Volunteer work

Volunteer work can be extremely useful for a startup business that needs to get its name known. "At the same time," say the Edwards, "you have to have firmly established boundaries in your own mind and clearly communicate that you are a business." The Edwards suggest that any volunteer work clearly state somewhere on it that the work is designed or printed by your desktop publishing firm. "Make it real clear, consistent with good taste, that you are a business that's providing that contribution."

Stephanie Hopkinson of Bellingham, Washington, had just started her desktop publishing business, Focal Point, when I interviewed her. At that point, her marketing efforts included volunteer work and posting flyers at the local university and community college, as well as passing out her business card "to everyone I meet."

Hopkinson said she's found networking more effective than anything else, but added that "volunteer work has brought me to the eyes of people more than any ad."

Established desktop publishing firms also find doing a certain amount of volunteer work good for business. Carol Pentleton, for example, also does "a decent amount of pro bono work. Often with the pro bono work, people want you to come up with the ideas. Volunteer projects tend to generate a fair amount of work."

# Cold calling

Cold calling takes a special kind of person, one who can take a lot of "no's" and rejection without letting it bother her or him. Consequently, for many of us cold calling, especially used by itself, is not effective. It does work for some, however. Jane Scarano is among those who's found it successful. "We have lists that we're working from. We're calling cold and setting up appointments. In the first sentence or two, we introduce ourselves as a computer-based graphic design firm that provides cost-effective solutions for clients' materials, that we can save clients a lot of money, and that we can provide services comparable to an ad agency and offer the client a significant savings."

## Finding clients through local printers

Developing good rapport with as many local printers as possible and learning the level and quality of service each printer offers, as well as their turnaround time, is really just another form of networking.

This can be done as a print broker, which has its good and bad points — the good point being that if you're willing to take the risk it can be extremely profitable, the bad being that if a job goes sour, or if you've acted on your client's behalf on good faith and the client refuses to pay, you can be left holding the bag for a sizable chunk of money that's owed the printer. It's not necessary, however, to be a print broker to maintain good relations with your area printers. Most printers will be more than happy to talk with you. While in some cases you may be competition for them, desktop publishing often is just a small part of a job that eventually must go on a press, and the printer realizes that either you or the client must take the job somewhere. By maintaining good relations with your local printers, if you have compatible equipment and software you also could be called upon to help out if they are suddenly swamped with more work than they can handle.

## Other local clients

In addition to printers, other local businesses are logical places to look for clients. Businesses and organizations that do not have newsletters are prime potential clients, as are those putting out newsletters that could use a professional touch. (Publishers of existing newsletters often find that when their time is factored in, it's less costly to hire a desktop publisher. As a bonus, their publications get a more professional look.) In most communities, the sheer number of restaurants offers DTPers another vast resource of potential clients — designing menus, if not advertisements.

# Other advertising

Some desktop publishers are advertising through electronic media. Lora Burgoon, for example, keeps an ad on Compuserve, and she's found at least one client through that ad. Becoming an active participant on electronic bulletin board forums also can help establish you as an authority, but it takes time, patience, and consistently knowledgeable responses.

# Other approaches

Some additional marketing techniques are being used effectively by DTPers. Charlene Anderson-Shea publishes a newsletter called *Newsletter Repair.* "Whenever I see a bad newsletter, I send one of these with a cover letter explaining to the client how I can help them improve for less money than they're spending."

Brochures and flyers can be effective marketing tools, but are best used to provide potential clients additional information once they've requested it, rather than as an initial direct mail piece.

Another way of marketing your services is by offering seminars or training. C.J. Metschke offers publishing productivity and other workshops. She views it as a way of building a good base income and "leveraging some of the things that I do. I think it's also a way to get other work. When I have done training, the people who brought me in to teach them how to do the newsletter often decide they don't really want to" spend the time doing it themselves, but would rather leave it to a professional.

# Newspaper advertising

I've purposely left newspaper advertising until last because of all the marketing methods mentioned during the course of interviewing, it's the one that desktop publishers unanimously reported was ineffective for finding clients. My own experience with several months of experimental advertising in my local daily bears this out.

The one exception I've found is specialized newsletters to a targeted market. Recently I placed an ad in *Writer's NW*, a publication geared specifically to writers, editors and educators involved with writing. I've had good response from the one ad, and plan to do more in future issues.

# This little piggy went to market...

For some of us marketing comes naturally. For others...well, let's just say we have to work at it (by the way, I fall into the latter category, though I like to think I'm better at it than when I purchased my first newspaper business). Metschke says of marketing, "I have not done a very good job of it. When I first started, because I had work, I was lulled into thinking I did not have to market. I would get big projects, have money, then spend two months lining up new work.

"Just recently, I've come to believe there are a lot of talented people but that there may be people with less talent who have more successful practices because of their marketing."

Metschke says she now is starting to identify potential clients and target a specific market, using the approach that she can help people solve problems. She's also using warm calling where "either I know someone directly or someone has given me a name, so I'm pretty likely to get a call back."

Once she's made the initial contact, Metschke says she talks to the prospect on the phone and pesters them for an interview. "I just want to make that process a little more systematic."

Jane Scarano also has experienced the cyclical marketing roller coaster. "If you're one person, it's hard to maintain marketing, sales, et cetera, and keep a high volume going if you're busy with production, which can be very time consuming. We find after finishing big projects that we don't have clients and we have to go back to marketing. In our case, we're considering hiring a part-time desktop publisher to come in and work here."

Graphic artist David Boe sees marketing as "a big black hole" for which he has no answers. "Everything I've ever done has been by referral. I can count on one hand the number of times I've had to go show a portfolio."

"You spend time marketing and selling, you take away time to produce," Boe says. "I haven't done any long-term marketing and in the long run, that may be detrimental. I haven't been bitten in the back yet, but I'm looking over my shoulder, waiting. Maybe I will get bitten in the back." At the same time, Boe admits that if he was interested in being more than a one-person business, part of his goal would be to do long-term marketing.

Not everyone finds marketing difficult, though. Judi Wunderlich, who operates a broker service for graphic arts freelancers in the Chicago area, says "marketing has come extremely easy for me. I haven't done any marketing in a year." She notes that she's marketing her service to a targeted audience. Since she deals only with people or companies that have their own art departments or studios, when she started her business she "opened up the Yellow Pages and input every single phone number and address of businesses that I knew might have a use for my services." These included advertising agencies, artists, graphic artists, desktop publishers, printers and typesetters.

Then she made up a mailer that was typeset and did a mailing. She didn't attempt, however, to mail to all 4,000 businesses whose names she had entered into her database. "I knew it would spell financial disaster if I attempted to market to 4,000 companies. Where would I get the capital to serve that many clients? Too much growth can kill a small business."

Kathleen Tinkel of Westport, Connecticut, has been a graphics designer for 30 years. Though she's never done much marketing or promotion herself, she's a firm believer in "marketing of specific kinds. If you're selling design services and, to a lesser extent, writing, there's a way this is personal work. I believe in personal marketing and getting to know people. Just don't drive yourself crazy going after a client when you have a personality conflict. It will probably never work."

# CHAPTER 3

# WHAT'S IN A NAME?

Ask an experienced retailer or real estate agent what's most important to a business' success and you'll hear, "Location, location, location."

Ask the same question of owners of a service-oriented business, though, and location's apt to be a secondary consideration since we can work anywhere, no matter who our clients or where they're located. Technological advances that have brought lower prices for computers, peripherals and other office equipment make this truer today than it was just a few years ago, and all indications are that this trend will continue. A good example is cellular phones. Though prices dropped steadily since they first came on the market, until late 1991 costs remained high enough that for many of us a cellular phone was still a luxury. Early in 1992, however, I saw two cellular phones advertised for less than a hundred dollars. One, a transportable, was advertised for $29. It's not unreasonable to expect that many cellular phones someday will be in this price range, just as once expensive "high-tech" pocket calculators and telephones now can be purchased by anyone with a few spare bucks.

On one hand, all this lower-priced technology is good because it means that many of us who previously could not afford to compete with big business can now do so effectively from the comfort of our own homes. On the other hand, anyone else who's so inclined can also afford the equipment, set up shop and offer the same services we do. Consequently, what becomes important to many clients is the level and quality of service offered.

For those of us who work in private industry, no matter what line of work we choose, there always will be those looking for a bargain at any price. At the same time, there are always those who insist on quality work from skilled craftsmen.

Desktop publishing is a skill demanding as much craft as that required of a wordsmith, a playwright or a shipwright. Certainly each requires at least slightly different skills but each also demands careful shaping and molding until the finished product fits together so well that only the closest analysis reveals any flaws. When desktop publishing was new, it drew a lot of attention from people who'd never before given any thought to how their printed materials were produced. Because of the "publishing" misnomer many, no doubt, saw it as the path to producing publications inexpensively in-house without ever needing a press. Indeed, some businesses now actually "desktop" jobs requiring thousands of pages and then photocopy them, even though it's generally far more cost effective to put such jobs on a press. Somehow, businesses like these are convinced they're saving money.

Unfortunately, as desktop publishing has evolved so has the public's perceptions and misconceptions about it, and the desktop publishing industry itself must shoulder much of the blame. To see why, all that's needed is a look at the diversity of jobs and services that fall under the desktop publishing umbrella. It covers everything from someone who simply produces a photocopied two-page newsletter using inexpensive software all the way to service bureaus and large corporations that are using all the latest technology and which have entire desktop publishing departments. Even within the large community of one- and two-person desktop publishers there's no standard. Ask several dozen desktop publishers to describe their businesses and each will give you a completely different answer. Often, the only similarities are the software or hardware used and even then there's sometimes no comparison.

It's no wonder the public and the general business community are confused. Take Joe, for example. He's a top real estate agent just down the road who wants to beef up his sales with an attractive four-color brochure that can be updated regularly as new houses come on the market. Through his network of contacts in the community, Joe knows several computer sales representatives and two desktop publishers.

Joe asks both of the desktop publishers for estimates and samples of work they've done previously. Joe understands a little bit about fonts and typography since he's done some advertising in the *Quantum Gazette,* the local daily. Just enough so that when the bids come back he doesn't ask either desktop publisher for any clarification or for more details about what's included and what's not. He asks for no clarification or breakdown of estimates for color printing estimates. Nevertheless, Joe sees by the samples that one desktop publisher's work is clearly superior to the other's even though their rates are about the same.

Meanwhile two computer sales representatives, who work on commission and also happen to sell software, have convinced Joe he can do the work himself and save a bundle of money. So Joe buys the software and soon finds himself spending 20 hours a week or better of his leisure time putting out his brochures. He quickly learns that, because his brochures use color photos and he needs large quantities, he still must pay to have them printed, and the photos never come out exactly right. Consequently, his brochure never has quite the feel that he wants to project to prospective home buyers. Before long, Joe's income drops off because he's not spending his time doing what he's good at — selling people their "dreams" through home ownership. Yet Joe can't put his finger on the problem, though he knows something's wrong.

If Joe's smart, and he must be to sell so many houses, he'll hire a good consultant who'll pinpoint the problem immediately and get Joe back on the right track by referring this work to desktop publishers, graphic artists and printers — people with expertise in this area.

Joe's problem should be the exception but unfortunately it's common and, along with shoddy work by some desktop publishers who charge high fees, it's a prime reason that desktop publishing's garnered a bad reputation in some circles. Of course, promoters of software or hardware as a "solution" to all costly printing jobs do nothing to help the cause either.

# The name game
## What is it you do?

Because desktop publishing is viewed so dimly by some, many who use desktop publishing technology have turned to describing services in other ways. A few come to mind: editorial consultant; communications consultant; newsletter publisher; graphic design, illustration and prepress production; graphic designer; multimedia marketing (use only if you truly offer multimedia services that are beyond desktop publishing technology); professional writing and design; electronic document design and prepress. Using a description other than "desktop publisher" really is as it should be (and as it should have been all along) since desktop publishing per se really is nothing more than electronic tools that can be used creatively for many types of printing-related jobs — publishing is something else entirely.

## The business of naming a business

Finding a way to describe services clearly in a few short words is only half of the name game, though. The other half is settling on a business name.

Naming a business can be simple. Anderson & Associates, for example, would project to potential clients a professional image and imply that I have others who work with me. Though calling the family dog an associate might be stretching it a bit, an associate could easily be my wife. Or kids. Or subcontractors. At least initially, it's not necessary for clients to know precise details of relationships with associates. Many business books and consultants favor this approach to naming a business. Of course, it's not going to work if you have a competitor that's already using the same or a similar name.

The other major drawback is that it requires clarification. By itself, Anderson & Associates does little beyond project a professional image.

For this reason and because desktop publishing by its nature usually requires use of at least a little imagination, I favor business names with creative flair that offer at least a hint of what the business is about.

Take the naming of my business, Writer's Bloc, for example. When I founded the company in mid-1989 I knew I wanted it to focus on the written word — writing, editing, design, manuscript preparation, prepress assistance, etc. — but I wanted to leave other avenues open as well. Additionally, the original concept included developing a core of established writers and editors available for assignments on a freelance basis — a bloc of writers with diverse specialties. This idea's still fluttering somewhere in my business plan and someday when time permits, I'll probably get started developing this network. Meanwhile, the odd spelling hasn't hurt business. Since the natural tendency is to put the "k" on the end of the word, potential clients immediately know that my main focus is on the written word. Since I do more than writing and editing, however, I settled on "communications consultant" as the broad term for what I do. Not ideal by any means, since it still requires explanation of services offered, but certainly better than the broader and nondescript term "desktop publisher."

My unique logo, which shows ink spilling from the inkwell of a quill pen and flowing into a computer monitor, subtly reinforces the emphasis on communications. Still, there are changes

# WRITER'S BLOC

I'd like to make. For example, I want to angle the copy coming from the computer terminal and list more of the services offered through the company.

Another example of business names that go beyond the basics are those used by Dennis & Linny Stovall. Their Media Weavers logo, for example, implies that they use various technologies to "weave" together a finished product that is more than the sum of its parts — careful crafting is implied. It also offers the flexibility of "weaving" publishing technologies with other media, including radio, television and multimedia on behalf of clients. The name and associated logo provide the service side of the Stovalls' business with a memorable presence in the marketplace.

For their own book publishing, and their company's principal name, they are Blue Heron Publishing. And though blue herons are found in temperate climates throughout the world, the bird is linked strongly to both the Pacific Northwest and the Far East. Thus Blue Heron Publishing projects to me an image of a publisher that cares about writers from the Pacific Northwest, but sees itself as part of the larger community of the Pacific Rim.

Blue Heron
Publishing, Inc

The Stovalls recommend that, unless you are a graphic artist, the expense of hiring one to design your logo and other graphic elements of your business image will be worth it.

# Getting it right the first time

Choosing a name becomes important early in the business process. A business name will be required if you apply for a business license, other permits or tax registration numbers that may be needed. Often, a search is required to be sure another business is not operating with the same or a similar name. It's sometimes possible to obtain licenses and permits with only a vague idea for business, but often agencies want specific information about a business and the goods or services it will offer.

Giving careful thought to a business name can speed the permit and licensing process but it adds another fringe benefit as an aside; it forces us to think about services offered and whether we ought to narrow or broaden our range of expertise to have the client base that we need. Too few services may limit our ability to draw enough of a client base to make it worth being in business; too many may spread us so thin that we can't do a good job at any of it.

A final serious consideration in the early selection of a name is that you will have to live with the one you choose. Once your market knows you by a name, it's difficult and expensive to change it or the image it projects.

# Tooting your own horn

As business owners, we need to be good at tooting our own horns, because nobody else is going to do it for us. It seems like this should come easily and naturally to anyone (especially desktop publishers) involved in communication. Foot-in-mouth disease strikes all too easily, though, and none of us is exempt — even good communicators. For example, I once commented early in a business ownership that we planned to run our competition out of town. The comment was intended as a joke but it wasn't taken that way by a store owner who was present, and things were difficult for us for several months after that.

Still, if you remember to keep the filter in place between brain and mouth, projecting the right business image and letting people know the services you offer isn't hard.

# In print

## LETTERHEAD

Business stationery is a good place to start. Many desktop publishers list their services as a part of their letterheads. Doctors, attorneys and other professionals are increasingly using this technique, and done tactfully it still projects a quality image.

## NEWSLETTERS

Useful, interesting newsletters offer another way to do self-promotion. To be most effective, a newsletter needs to address a target audience — doctors or attorneys, for example — with information useful to that specific audience. Instead of touting the benefits of using your service, for example, include an article about how Dr. Jones' practice benefits from a regularly published newsletter; another about why design is such an important element when dealing with printed material. By all means, include information on how the recipient can get more information but keep it in perspective with the rest of the newsletter. If anything, understatement is better than using type or graphics that call attention to themselves.

## BROCHURES

Brochures and pamphlets are wonderful tools for self-promotion when used in conjunction with other marketing methods. I don't recommend them for an initial mailing but they're wonderful for giving to potential clients who request more information. A company with a variety of services can keep several on hand, each describing a different service or combination of services.

This approach allows marketing of specific services to target audiences. Its drawback is that once a client is using one service, we want them to also use other services but since we've provided service-specific brochures, the client may be unaware of all we offer.

Everything about your brochure tells the prospect something about your services. Design, focus, text, graphics, printing and even paper are part of the message. Good design can be learned, emulated, or purchased; clear focus results from your well-developed business plan; effective, concise text draws on your writing abilities or can be bought; appropriate graphics may be your forté or the work of another artist; quality printing is a matter of careful selection, but is readily available; and well-designed brochure papers are available in small quantities at prices that make it affordable for even small desktop publishing businesses to produce attractive documents.

### BUSINESS CARDS

These are probably the ultimate self-promotion tool but I'd never rely on a business card alone for promoting a business. No doubt some end up in Rolodexes or on desks, as intended, but too many end up in shirt pockets or underneath a car seat. An exception may be the plastic business cards designed specifically for Rolodexes and made to last indefinitely, but these cost considerably more than a standard business card.

Beware trying to put too much on your card. It's better to have several targeted cards than to clutter one and risk appearing to be a "jack of all trades, master of none."

# Over the phone and in person

Even if we're good at explaining our services in print, answering questions that come in over the phone may not come naturally to us. Listening to a good sales rep on the phone, or to someone who's been trained in telemarketing, it sounds easy to sell a client on services. For many of us, though, myself included, answering questions over the phone about services doesn't come naturally.

Many experienced businesspeople recommend using a script with answers to the most frequently answered questions. Another technique that works equally as well when it's impossible to provide pat answers over the phone is to have a list of questions within arm's reach to ask the client. In either case, rehearsing the information is recommended so that it doesn't come across to the client that either you don't know your business or you're presenting canned information.

When practical, a face-to-face meeting to discuss services offers the best approach to meeting with someone who has a lot of questions.

# CHAPTER 4

# THE PRICE OF DOING BUSINESS

Probably no other area of desktop publishing stirs more discussion and disagreement than setting fees. Do you charge an hourly rate? A flat fee? By the page? Do you use a combination of these, or some other method? There's no "right" answer, and how you charge will depend in part on how you view your business and the services you offer. Nevertheless, following some basic guidelines will ensure a business that is structured to make a profit.

Many books about general business principles offer precise formulas for determining how much you should charge. Rather than offer fixed formulas, we're going to explore the underlying principles behind these formulas and take a look at fee-setting through various desktop publisher's comments.

## Beginner's syndrome

Service businesses can fall into two common traps when setting fees. Since new businesses tend to be most vulnerable to these traps, I like to lump them together in what I call "beginner's syndrome." The first "trap" is charging only the hourly rate you want to earn, the second is undercutting your competition's charges with no firm or reasoned basis for doing so. The problem with both approaches is that they don't take into account obvious or hidden overhead. Even if you work from home, you have some obvious business overhead beyond what you want to earn. Examples are extra electricity to power a computer, laser printer and other peripherals; the cost of an additional phone line or two to accommodate business and fax needs; and acquisition of business software. Hidden or less obvious overhead can include business mileage, the need to set aside funds for equipment and software upgrades and replacement of vehicles, and budgeting for unbillable time. Some costs, such as long distance calls, can fall into either category, depending on how and whether charges are billed back to a customer. Other costs enter the picture, too: federal, state and local taxes, social security, retirement funds.

In my years in business, I've seen many small businesses charge only what the owners felt they deserved in an hourly wage. In many cases even home-based businesses using this approach didn't last long. Those that survived usually did so because business owners realized their folly and made some adjustments. "When we first started," say Dennis and Linny Stovall, owners of Blue Heron Publishing, Inc. in Hillsboro, Oregon, "like most people we tended to underprice ourselves because we were hungry and we wanted the work. Now, we have two ways of pricing, depending on the job: we get all the prices and add a markup to the job, or we charge by the hour for work we do."

"Our billing changed," says Dennis, "when we began to realize we were getting petty little jobs that nickel and dimed us. We began raising our rates but we didn't lose any cash. We got better clients, and clients who were more understanding of the value they got.

"If you charge too little, you get what you charge for...too little."

Like many owners of small business do, the Stovalls started

out undercapitalized. They borrowed money from family and were fortunate to find a banker who knew Linny from an earlier job. Later, however, another banker at the same institution called the loan "because we were small publishers, and publishing is considered a high-risk business." Today, desktop publishing services generate a large part of the Stovalls' cash flow, carrying them through the long-haul cash flow cycles of book publishing.

Some desktop publishers realize they don't use the best fee-setting methods. Don Hinkle of The Village Edit, Green Village, New Jersey, for example, says "I pretty much let the client tell me how much she or he has to pay for a job, then I decide if I can do it for that. My wife is a much better biller than I am. She sets a hefty per hour price and always sets half again as many hours as I would set aside for the same job and always gets the amount she names. I think people inherently trust her.

"I have one client who thinks he's paying me $7.50 an hour to word process his letters for him. He's an elderly fella and I haven't had the courage to tell him I can't live on that, so I do the letters and then bill him what I think the job is worth and he pays it. But still, I usually end up doing it for about $12–15. I'm trying to find someone else to take on his work for him so I won't feel like I have to do it."

Undercutting the competition is another mistake that can prove fatal to business. In interviewing for this book, I came across two businesses — one relatively new, the other established — that used this approach. In one case, the business owner told me that the going rate in the nearest East Coast metropolitan area was $50 an hour, "so I chop $20 an hour off that. Depending on the level of work I'm doing, I'll charge less than the hourly rate. To me, I don't think it's right to charge someone $30 an hour if I'm simply typing as opposed to doing design and layout." In the other case, the business owner cited fees charged by a phototypesetter for whom some part-time work had been done as a basis for determining rates. "Most of what he did I felt could be adequately and efficiently done with desktop publishing at at least half the price."

If there's a sound basis for doing so, it's one thing to lower your rates because it's all the market will bear. It's another to do so without considering the overall effect this will have on business profitability. Both businesses cited here may be showing a profit, but by using this approach, the owners may unknowingly be limiting their income potential.

"I am concerned about people who underprice their work," says Heidi Waldmann, owner of Choice Words & Graphics in St. Paul, Minnesota. "I'm concerned not from the standpoint of competition, but from their not understanding the realities" of business. When it comes to setting rates, Waldmann's a firm believer in talking with an accountant or tax preparer and with people who have been in the business awhile.

She also cites her own experience with lower rates. "I found that when I undercharged, people didn't take me seriously. It was like I was clerical help, I wasn't treated as a professional. When my rates went up, people started seeing me as a professional and clients respected my time a lot more."

Rick Ornberg & Associates in Des Plaines, Illinois, provides "complete desktop publishing services, producing several regular newsletters, brochures, direct mail pieces, logo design and, within the past three or four years, considerable political campaign literature ranging from national congressional candidates, gubernatorial races, state congressional, down through local aldermanic races and school referendums." Says Ornberg, "As for rates, I've established a starting point figure for newsletter production on a per page basis, beginning at $125 a page. Added to that are typesetting costs ($30–45 per page), disk storage charges, and so forth. On many jobs not fitting the rate scale, I fall back on a minimum $45 to $55 per hour rate plus materials. If I broker printing, I tack on the standard 17 percent or at times more (depending on hassle factors). "Color slide generation can bring from $25 to $85 plus, depending on complexity."

Jim Dornbos, owner of a traditional commercial printing company in Saginaw, Michigan, that also offers desktop publishing services says "typically you find the guy in the printing business who sets up a business in a garage doesn't appreciate all that goes into expenses. He might charge $10 for something I charge $20 for, but he doesn't see those extra expenses. You always face that person who, in the short term, is making you look bad when you can venture a guess that it's probably costing you both about the same amount of money.

"I look at those who are working from home and charging less than $30 an hour and they either have another job or they're not taking into account their overhead," says Dornbos.

My wife and I purchased our first newspaper business in 1984. Though the city was small, we faced competition from another newspaper and I'm the first to admit that I almost fell into this trap of undercutting the competition on prices. Fortunately, I got some advice from a publisher who'd been in the business far longer than I and I took a second, third, and even fourth look at the effects this would have. No matter how I looked at it, my final analysis clearly showed that we could not make a profit by undercutting the competition. Instead, we decided to focus on service and we settled on a rate comparable to, if not slightly above, that of our competition.

## Setting your rates

Some desktop publishers are most comfortable charging an hourly rate, others a flat fee, still others on a sliding scale, and some by a per page rate. There are advantages and disadvantages to each and some good reasons that it can pay to remain flexible on how clients are billed. Clients, such as attorneys, are often comfortable with an hourly rate, since that's how they bill; other prospective clients may prefer being quoted flat-fee estimates; and on some jobs, you may prefer to bill expenses separately, or it may make sense in particular cases to incorporate them into the bid.

But regardless of how clients are ultimately invoiced, we all need a starting point in determining our rates. Whether you use an established fee-setting formula or determine fees on an informal basis, a good starting point is what you'd like to earn. Determine this on whatever basis feels comfortable: annual, monthly, or hourly. Add to this figure benefits, taxes, and overhead costs, including such things as office supplies. Include set-aside funds for retirement, equipment and vehicle replacements and upgrades, and software purchases. Also consider and build into your price structure unbillable time — those inevitable hours that cannot be charged to clients.

Regardless of how they bill or how they arrive at their rates, somewhere along the line most desktop publishers convert their final figure into an hourly rate that is used at least loosely as a guideline for setting fees. The ultimate charge may be a flat fee or a per page charge, but chances are that if it's been arrived at from a business perspective, somewhere along the line an hourly rate came into play.

Obviously, a desktop publisher who's satisfied with an annual salary of $15,000 a year and no benefits will arrive at a much different figure than one who wants to earn $50,000 a year with full benefits and money set aside for retirement. On the other hand, unless we're independently wealthy and operating a desktop publishing business for fun, how many of us can get by in today's society on $15,000 a year? And if we are independently wealthy, why would we want to assume some of the legal risks associated with desktop publishing (see chapters 10 and 11) for a meager $15,000 a year?

# Where has the time gone?

If you're like me, you find yourself asking that question a lot when you've finished a job for a client and it's taken longer than expected. Some of us are innately better at tracking our time and expenses than others. I'm not, especially when it comes to using paper and pencil to keep track. I make the notes, all right, but they promptly get lost in the shuffle of paperwork on my desk and when it comes time to bill, charges and expenses that should be billed have gone the way of the wayward wind.

Fortunately for me, and others like me, help is as close as a good time- and expense-tracking software package. Time and expense software may not be for everyone, but odds are that even many who are good at keeping manual records can benefit from such software. "We keep track of expenses, charges to clients, et cetera, in a Day-Timer," say the Stovalls, "but tracking time and expenses are areas that we probably could do better at. However, we have gotten our bids to the point where we're accurately building in a reasonable profit while being competitive."

Ornberg reports, "I have yet to try any software to control my billing. My weakest link in business is having the proper discipline to intelligently monitor my time on task."

Several inexpensive money management programs are on the market, as well as some more expensive but also more versatile software for tracking time and expenses. Using some of this software is "as easy as writing a check," say authors Paul and Sarah Edwards, "so there's not a good reason for, with minimal effort, keeping extremely good records."

Of the dozens of people I interviewed, most were using accounting software but only about a half dozen reported using any time and expense software. One reason for this, I suspect, is that there's a substantial learning curve for some of the best time and expense software packages. For example, I've been using my time and expense software for about a year. A couple of others interviewed use this same program. All of us who use it found the initial setup "non-intuitive." I'm generally a quick study with new software, but I found the learning curve for this program to be several months, partly because of its tremendous flexibility.

The trade-off is that I have a program that allows me to bill one client on an hourly rate, another on a strictly time basis, another on a time and expense basis and still others by flat fees, with a variety of flat-fee options such as minimum or maximum flat fee and inclusion or exclusion of expenses. Additionally, it gives me one of the best accounts receivable packages I've ever seen for small business, client histories with just a couple of keystrokes, accurate tracking of time and expenses with the option of billing these or not, and the option of billing by my rate, by a rate established specifically for a client, or by an activity. I've also used it with reasonable accuracy to estimate time and expenses for projects. Of course, the software's effectiveness is only as good as the information that's entered and if you forget about a key expense, you'll still be out that money. However, once you've entered a type of activity or expense, it's always there for future reference. A quick glance at these lists can serve as a helpful reminder to bill an expense that otherwise might be overlooked. Finally, once I've done enough jobs of a particular type, I'll be able to offer accurate estimates, with allowances for variations or variables.

## Put time on your side

Aside from making it easier to track time and expense charges to clients, one of the biggest advantages to good time and expense software is its billing capabilities, not only in the ways already mentioned but also in ease of billing. The best programs allow you to bill immediately upon completion of a job and post to general ledgers from many popular accounting programs. Or bill a project in stages. Or expenses separately. Now, instead of waiting until the end of the month you can finish a project for client A on the ninth and bill it that day or the next, another project for client B on the 23rd and bill it immediately, and so on. Or you can finish two projects for client A — one on the ninth, another on the 17th and bill both immediately on completion or wait and bill them both together, all without affecting how you choose to bill other clients. You can bill expenses as they're incurred, holding the client's invoice for the actual work until the project's completion.

All this leads, in theory at least, to better cash flow. After all, if you can send your invoice out sooner, you stand a better chance of collecting what's owed you sooner.

# Choosing time and expense software

Look for several things in time and expense software:

- Ease of use. Usually we want software that's easy to use and quick to learn. When it comes to time and expense software, though, I think a longer learning curve pays off and leads to long-term ease of use.
- Will the software run as a memory resident program?
- If you're tracking time charges, does it allow you to track two or more projects simultaneously and will it keep track of time on projects even when your computer is shut off?
- How easy is it to make adjustments if you find an error in time or expense charges?
- Does it have a built-in timer and also allow you to enter time and expenses manually?
- What kinds of reports can you generate? Does it allow you to create custom reports? At the very least, you should be able to create reports about the status of clients' funds (withdrawals, deposits, payments to or from a client's account); list all billed and unbilled transactions; and obtain summary reports for such things as billable vs. unbillable time.
- Can your report data be converted to easy-to-understand bar and pie graphs?
- How flexible are the billing options? Do you have flexibility in positioning billing messages? Can you view the bill layout as you're creating it?
- What kind of password security system is there?
- How many clients can the software handle, and how many projects per client?
- Finally, as always, what kind of technical support does the company vending the time and expense software offer?

# CHAPTER 5

# BACK TO BASICS

When we purchased our first business, I knew little about business basics. I knew customers were billed and, as a consumer, I knew about paying interest on account balances that were over 30 days. I didn't know what receivables or payables were, nor that the standard abbreviations for these common business terms were A/R and A/P. I naively assumed that all customers would pay their bills on time, or at least close to it; that we'd be able to do all of our own bookkeeping and that for the balance finding a CPA would be a breeze. I knew nothing about the amount of paperwork that state and federal agencies required from employers for payroll and other taxes and unemployment insurance nor the frequency with which this paperwork had to be filed.

If we'd known which questions to ask and which agencies to turn to, we could have learned many of these things ahead of time. We also could have looked to business books from our local library. Even in the mid-1980s, however, there were not the vast resources that are available today to new businesses and their owners. Far more business books can be found today, opening the door to a wider range of views on the best ways to conduct business; electronic bulletin board and database services are better organized and offer more resources today than back then; business consultants and financial advisors are a phone call away.

Today, my wife and I have separate home-based businesses that incorporate much of what we learned through involvement in our first two ventures. Still, for anyone who has the choice, I don't recommend starting the way we did. Baptism by fire's all right if you like the challenge of conducting business by the seat of your pants, with only a vague idea of where you're headed or why. With all the resources available today, there are better ways to prepare for business ownership.

# Doing business with business

Most independent desktop publishers prefer to concentrate on doing business with businesses, since they tend to need more printed material, more often, than individuals. Yet many of these same desktop publishers report using payment methods that can prevent a business from reaching its full potential. Here in the Pacific Northwest, for example, one of the unspoken and unwritten rules is that if you want to do business with business you offer terms, the standard being payment within 30 days. An amazing number of desktop publishers throughout the country reported requiring payment of from one-third to fifty percent before they would start work on a project, with the balance due on delivery of the job.

From the perspective of a one-person business that can't afford to lose money, this seems to make sense. After all, it reduces your risks and you've ensured payment before you're well into a project, only to find out that you're not going to get paid. A closer examination of such policy reveals some problems, though. First, if you live in an area where businesses are accustomed to paying on terms and if there are other desktop publishers in the area, chances are you'll lose clients to competitors who are willing to offer terms. Secondly, larger companies almost always offer terms to clients, so requiring deposits and payment upon delivery for even small jobs is a good way of tipping a prospective client that you're a small operation. With the billing software available today, small home-based companies can effectively compete with big business. In fact, we have an advantage that big business often lacks: we can offer a level of personal service unheard of in most large companies. So why risk doing anything that's going to let our clients know we're a small operation, if we feel it will make or break a sale?

Finally, consider that some businesses will interpret failure to offer terms a sign that you really don't want their business. Use of good credit checking techniques (see chapter 7) will reduce the risks you assume in offering credit, at the same time offering potential for increased revenue and more profit.

I don't advocate offering terms in every situation. Even in our first businesses, there were times when we required substantial deposits because of the amount of money involved in completing a project. Any time we had jobs that involved large printing bills or other major expenses and a third party was involved in the project, say a printer, we always required enough of a deposit so that if the job fell through after the project was on the press we had at least covered our expenses. We also required payment on delivery if such a project was for an individual; for businesses, it depended on credit history and what kind of payment history the business had with us.

We had one major exception to offering terms: any time we did work for political candidates, it was cash up front before we'd even start on the work. Not all desktop publishers do work for political candidates, but most of those who do report similar policies. Rick Ornberg of Ornberg & Associates, for example, insists "on at least the printing costs up front from one and all political clients." With that exception, for established clients he bills net 30 days upon completion of services.

The reasons for collecting in advance from political candidates are simple. Political campaigns last only as long as the election and it can be difficult to track down a campaign's finance manager once an election is over. Not all political campaigns are well-financed; more than one political campaign has been known to incur debts far beyond its means of paying. Not all candidates who lose do so graciously; a poor loser often is not of a mood to pay bills run up during a campaign.

One way that some home-based businesses get around the problem of offering terms is by accepting VISA and Mastercard. The client still gets terms but the desktop publisher gets paid. The trade-off, of course, is that the desktop publisher also pays a discount for the privilege of accepting the credit card. Problems with home-based businesses getting set up to accept VISA and Mastercard are covered well in some of Paul and Sarah Edwards' books and in other business books, so I'll just mention here that it can be difficult.

## Accounts receivable

Accounts receivable are nothing more than the business term for the amount of money extended to clients on credit. The term can apply to amounts owed by individual clients or businesses, as well as to the total amount owed to your business through purchase of goods or services on credit. Accounts receivable are treated as a business asset representing claims against future collection from clients who owe you money. For companies that extend terms to clients, accounts receivable provide one of the best tools for monitoring cash flow. If most clients are paying within the customary 30 days, it's a healthy sign that money is flowing into your business as it should. If a lot of accounts start taking 60 days or more to pay, it's time to take a look at what's happening. The causes may be external — a downturn in the economy; local, regional, national or world events that are beyond your control; or even something simple, such as a change in federal, state or local tax structures. Or the causes may be internal: have you said or done something to offend a wide number of clients; has there been a change in company policy that's resulted in unanticipated negative side effects; has there been a change in the quality or level of service provided by your company; do you have a new salesperson who's making claims that can't be backed up by the service you can offer or who's promising terms or conditions that can't be met? Any of these things affect how your business is perceived in the business community as a whole, and any of them can effect how quickly you'll be paid.

It's not until accounts get over 90 days, though, that you should start worrying that you might not get paid at all. Any business that offers terms is bound to have a few accounts that end up in the 90-day or over category. That's one of the risks of doing business. If you suddenly start finding a lot of accounts over 90 days, though, it's a sign that something's seriously wrong. Even at this stage, many businesspeople can analyze the situation and pinpoint one or two things that may be the root cause of the problem. If you can't, there's certainly nothing wrong with seeking the advice of financial experts, whether it be a CPA, a business consultant or a financial adviser with business expertise.

What's been mentioned to this point about collecting on receivables is the ideal. The reality is that it sometimes takes longer to collect than this ideal. Paul and Sarah Edwards, for example, urge approaching the whole billing issue "on an extremely businesslike basis." They have a policy of invoicing within 24 hours of completing a project. Still, when dealing with big corporations that are playing cash flow games, it can take well over 30 days to receive payment.

Governmental agencies are one notable exception to generalizations about offering terms. Though notoriously slow at paying bills, they do eventually pay and rarely with any quibbling about the amount billed. Few governmental agencies pay within 30 days. Many pay within 60, but in some cases it can be 90 days or longer before payment is received.

Incidentally, most desktop publishers interviewed who work on an accounts receivable basis reported few problems with getting paid by clients.

## Charging Interest

Incredible as it sounds, some businesses never charge interest on past due accounts. The prevailing argument from them seems to be that nobody pays it anyway and it creates a lot of extra bookkeeping, so why charge it? I don't look at it that way. For starters, I'm not a bank so why should I loan someone my money interest-free for as long as they'd like to take to repay me? That's essentially what I'd be doing. As for extra bookkeeping, with today's software this should be a minor problem and while interest often isn't paid, my experience is that when people know it's being charged, they pay their bills quicker.

## Building Business Value

Since accounts receivable are a tangible asset on a business' balance sheet they can help strengthen a company's value. That's another reason I'm amazed at the number of desktop publishers who said they do not offer terms to clients. Sure, cash also is an asset on a balance sheet but a company that shows both cash and receivables may find it easier to obtain a bank loan than the company with only cash.

Receivables strengthen a firm in another way, too. Desktop publishing is a relatively new industry and most of us are involved in it because we enjoy it. Sooner or later, however, some of us will find that we want out of our businesses. Maybe a better opportunity's come along, or there's been a death in the family. Whatever the reason, it's time to move on.

One way to get out of business is to simply close the doors and quit. Depending on the legal structure of your business and regulations in your state, this can be expensive. A more sensible way, if the option's available, is to sell the business. A business with tangible assets is worth far more to a purchaser than a business with only intangible assets, such as goodwill. Selling a home-based desktop publishing business may prove difficult to start with, but if it has no tangible assets other than a computer and a few peripherals it may be nearly impossible.

## Accounts payable

Accounts payable is nothing more than the business term for what a business owes for goods or services extended on credit. Payables are treated as a liability on income statements and balance sheets. Payables also represent another side of cash flow and thus another means of monitoring.

Just as with home finances, ideally we'd always have more cash coming into a business than going out. In theory, as long as sales are exceeding expenses this is the case. Often it is.

But not always.

Many businesses can show hefty accounts receivable sums among their assets, yet when you look at liabilities they're not paying all their bills. Sometimes this can be because a company just bought a major piece of equipment or the company simply is overextended, but it also can be a strong indicator that cash, though on the books, simply is not flowing into the business as it should. It may mean that more attention needs to go to collecting receivables or that review of credit policy is needed.

### ALSO BUILDING BUSINESS VALUE

It may seem strange that a liability also can strengthen a business financially. However, when a banker can see that payments are being made regularly against payables, it says a lot about your management of a business.

# Dangers of growth

Unless we're in business solely for fun (or we want a business to incur loss as a tax write-off against another profitable business), we all want our businesses to grow. After all, at least part of the reason for owning a business is to have the opportunity to make more money than we could working for someone else.

# Making business grow

Sounds simple enough. It could even be a catchy slogan for a business consultant.

But wait. There's a catch.

Too much growth, too fast, can kill a business.

Now wait a minute, I can hear you asking yourself. First I say that we all want business growth, and now I'm saying that growth actually cannot only be bad for business but that it can put you out of business.

That's right. That's what I said.

Consider this scenario:

Joe publishes a small weekly newspaper in rural Maple Falls. Though the town's one major employer, a timber mill, has just re-opened the town's economy remains stagnant. Residents drive to nearby Megacity to purchase many of their goods and services, even though most of these same goods and services can be purchased locally at a slightly higher price. Since Joe does no outside printing for customers, his sole income comes from revenues generated by the newspaper.

With a stagnant economy, Joe finds it tougher to sell advertising space in his newspaper. He begins looking for other revenue sources. He starts several new publications, such as a visitor's guide and a car care guide. He also begins offering desktop publishing services both within the community and via modem to customers throughout the country.

To do all this, Joe needs to invest $5,000 in equipment. No problem. He has the cash for some of the purchases and his credit with vendors and suppliers is good.

Being reasonably good at marketing, Joe has no problem promoting these new services and the jobs roll in.

So far so good.

Joe never experienced cash flow problems before and he doesn't expect any now. After all, business is better than ever. Suddenly, however, the company begins having severe cash flow problems. The underlying problem is simple. Business is indeed better than ever. In order to provide the additional service, however, Joe has to buy more supplies in larger quantities than before. Not all of Joe's new clients pay their bills promptly but Joe's payment terms to his creditors are still the same. He finds the company paying out money to creditors long before it is received from clients.

Or this scenario:

Lisa, a resident of Megacity, has an idea for a unique desktop publishing service that will cater to pet owners and veterinarians. Since she'll operate this service from home, Lisa plans to remain a one-person business. Lisa grabs her Megacity phone book, sits down at her computer and enters into her database the names of all veterinarians, pet stores, kennels, horse stables, and other suppliers of animal care goods and services. When she's done, Lisa has entered the names, addresses and phone numbers of more than 3,000 businesses.

Lisa does a bulk mailing to all of these businesses at one time, using up all but $2,000 of her capital. Then she gets on the phone and starts making follow-up phone calls. Lisa gets a 2.5 percent favorable response to her marketing efforts and suddenly she has 75 clients. Eighteen of these clients want major projects such as a book or brochure.

Before she started, Lisa realized the importance of prompt service to clients. Figuring that she could need help with some of the workload, Lisa lined up three other desktop publishers at $15 an hour each on a temporary, as needed basis. With 75 clients, there is enough work to keep all four busy for several months.

Each of the three temporary desktop publishers works 20-hour weeks and wants payment every two weeks. At the end of the first two weeks, Lisa owes them $1,800. Lisa offered terms to all of her clients, figuring it would help build business.

Fortunately for Lisa, several smaller jobs were worked in among the larger ones and many clients paid promptly. Lisa is able to meet her $1,800 payroll and add to the $200 that remained of her capital. But her business is off to a shaky start and problems collecting from even one or two accounts could be enough to put her out of business, if she can't find loans to cover her payables.

## Plan for growth

In the two hypothetical cases cited here, the business owners simply tried to grow too fast and did not consider all the effects that sudden, uncontrolled growth would have on their businesses. Planned growth, on the other hand, can be a boon to any business.

A plan doesn't need to be rigid; it should allow for changes in technology and circumstances. Tools for achieving rational growth include

- a solid, written business plan (or at the very least a firm idea of where your business is headed);
- use of sound management practices, including cash flow analysis and projections (specialty software is available for this or you can use a spreadsheet); and
- use of sound accounting principles.

It's potential situations like the two mentioned here that make me nervous when there's little in the way of receivables on my books, and I'm not alone in that thinking. Says Heidi Waldmann of Choice Words & Graphics, St. Paul, Minnesota, "I can have thousands in my bank account, but if my receivables are down it makes me nervous. I am happiest when most of my bills are paid, I don't have a lot of cash on hand, and I have a ton of receivables. That makes me a whole lot happier than having a whole lot of cash on hand and not a lot of receivables. It's easy to spend money on equipment and needs and forget that I have regular bills to pay."

## Collecting on receivables

A business always faces the possibility of making collection efforts any time it holds receivables. To me, the fear of having some receivables eventually show up in the bad debt column is not sufficient reason to require a pay-as-you-go policy from all clients.

For one thing, chances are good that if I've extended credit and I expect the amount owed to be large, I've done a reasonable amount of checking. It's still no guarantee that I'll be paid, but it's likely I will. On the other hand, if the amount I'll bill is small, I often go with my "gut feeling" and give the client credit. If I have a problem collecting, I discuss it with the client before doing another job. Admittedly, this is a "small-town" approach but it works well for me. What it boils down to, I think, is that in today's fast-paced and high-pressure society people are pleasantly surprised to find a business that's willing to offer that trust.

## The friendly reminder

When collection efforts are necessary, in my experience the best first step is a simple reminder. This can be in the form of a reminder on an invoice (but use an ink color other than red, which has too many symbolic overtones) or, depending on how well you know your client, a phone call or a personal visit. In my experience, a personal face-to-face meeting with the client usually achieves the best results. When first working with a new client, I always give them the benefit of doubt. After all, few of us can honestly say that we've *never* forgotten to pay a bill. It happens.

Whether it's stated or not, if it's obvious that a client is having difficulty I'll work out a payment arrangement that's mutually acceptable. In some cases, I've even been known to accept items on trade in lieu of a cash payment. I acquired two desks that way a few years back. Sure, I'd have preferred the cash, but at the same time I got items I needed and was able to clear a long overdue account without it affecting the client's credit and making an enemy for life. Since we lived in a small, rural community at the time, this was important. With this same client, the business also bought gasoline on terms, and we deducted the amount we owed from what was owed us.

I've dealt with slow paying restaurants by going in, ordering a meal, and then saying, when presented with the bill, "Gee, I'd really like to pay our tab, but I can't until you pay yours." This often works in small towns.

# Harsher means

Sometimes polite ways of asking bring no results, or payments are sparse and scattered over a period of months. At this point, it's time to consider more drastic actions: collection agencies, an attorney, or small claims court.

## COLLECTION AGENCIES

If you have a lot of receivables and a fair amount of them end up in your over 90-day column, using a collection agency may make sense. We used an agency in our first business, only briefly at our second. Agency's payment structures vary, but often there is a base fee that covers a set number of collections or a predetermined dollar amount. Once this fee is paid, you refer accounts to the agency for collection. The agency usually keeps a percentage of what it collects, often about 50 percent. This might sound steep, but if an agency does collect on your behalf, you've just received 50 percent of what otherwise would have been nothing.

Drawbacks of collection agencies are that many collection efforts are not effective and if you have only a few or only occasional overdue accounts or the amounts owed you are small, it can be costly to go this route. An agency may agree to work on behalf of your firm, but that's no guarantee it will be able to collect.

## ATTORNEYS

Many attorneys will write collection letters, demanding payment for overdue amounts. Some do this on a contingency basis so that you pay when and if a collection effort succeeds, others require payment before writing the letter. As with collection agencies, there is no guarantee that an attorney's collection letter will bring results. Unless the amount owed is large, odds are that the matter won't be pursued through a costly court system. Still, a demanding letter from an attorney sometimes scares people into paying.

## SMALL CLAIMS COURT

Over the past couple of years, I've talked with several business owners who are taking nonpaying clients to small claims court. Rules vary from locale to locale, but small claims courts usually can hear only cases below a certain dollar amount and some types of cases cannot be heard in small claims court regardless of dollar amounts involved. Judges in many small claims courts are sympathetic to the problems of small business and, if well-documented evidence is presented, the chances are good of getting a favorable ruling. Of course, getting a judgment is still no guarantee that you'll be paid, but I suspect most people pay up when a ruling is against them, unless they simply don't have the money.

# Cash flow and marketing

Though many businesses treat cash flow and marketing separately, the two really are closely related. Without good cash flow, the money won't be available for special promotions and advertising. Without advertising and promotions it's difficult for a business to grow, or sometimes even to maintain the status quo. Marketing, though only one part of the total business structure and often emphasized to the point of overshadowing other crucial areas, is essential to produce good cash flow. Without adequate sales, there's not enough revenue to operate the company. Without money to run the company, a business dies.

Good cash flow management and effective marketing strategies feed on each other, serving to strengthen the other. The key is to juggle all the pieces of the business puzzle without ever letting one drop to the ground.

# Barters and trades

If they're honest about it, nearly all businesses would have to admit to some level of bartering and trading of goods or services. Many businesses, however, will tell you that they never barter or trade.

So if most businesses barter or trade to some degree, why do so many say they don't? I'm not sure there's any one answer, but we can look at some possibilities. First, and probably foremost, the IRS considers barters and trades taxable. So even if no money is received for goods or services, both parties are expected to place dollar values on the goods or services and report the amounts as taxable items. Secondly, I suspect that sometimes such barters and trades are conducted informally and there's never any spoken request by either party for such services. In other words, the goods or services are an implied part of a deal that's beneficial to both parties — "you rub my back and I'll rub yours." Finally, informal barters and trades can be good for business. A favor done today for a friend or even a competitor can reap big dividends later.

# CHAPTER 6

# PENNIES IN YOUR POCKETS

As incredible as it seems, some desktop publishers say they've never had a problem client. My first thought when someone tells me that is that the businessperson is either incredibly lucky or hasn't been in business long. I also hope he or she has taken the time to prepare for the worst while apparently dealing with the best in the way of clients.

## Picky clients and "profitless" customers

Guide Joe Want used to say about Alaska's grizzlies and Kodiak brown bears that only one bear in ten is a troublemaker but you don't know whether that one bear will be the first bear you meet or the last. If you're incredibly lucky, you may not meet a troublemaking bear out of the first fifty or sixty you come across, maybe the first hundred. Or maybe you'll never meet one. But it pays to be ready just in case.

It works the same way with clients. Difficult clients come in all sizes and shapes, some with pocketloads of money that they'd prefer to keep but that they'll grudgingly part with if you jump through all the right hoops. Their hoops, not yours. And you never know from the moment you first hang out a shingle whether a troublesome client will be your first client or your last — or any in between.

It's impossible in a book this length to list all potential problem areas with clients, but we can look at some of the most common.

## UNREALISTIC CLIENT EXPECTATIONS

Probably the most common of any problem discussed here, it often goes hand in hand with people who are looking for a bargain and people who consider themselves design "experts" even though they've never spent a day of their lives learning anything about any type of publishing work.

Charles C. Montgomery of Design for Print Studio in Richmond, Virginia, tries to educate clients who fall into this category, but admits that "some can't be educated." Some people have decided that desktop publishing is simple secretarial work, Montgomery notes. "Their minds seem to be made up. You really can't convince them that there's more to it than they think."

Client expectations that can lead to problems include:

- Making unlimited changes at all stages of proofing, including bluelines, at the price quoted in the original estimate;
- Expecting as much time to be spent on their four-page newsletter as is spent on a major book project;
- Expecting deadlines to be met when copy is brought in a day or more later than it's been promised or, worse yet, the day before a project is scheduled for completion.
- Expecting to be billed at normal rates for a project that requires rapid turnaround at the client's request.

- Failure to understand computer technology and its limits. "I hate working with a client who doesn't understand computerization," says Ron Wodaski, a former journalist turned desktop publisher in Pittsburgh, Pennsylvania. "No amount of education is going to change the client's concept that because it's computerized, it should be easy. This leads to unrealistic expectations. About half the time, I just turn the job down. It's usually a loser."

- Thinking that desktop publishing has replaced all other steps in the printing process. Usually this is a problem with clients who think that the printing process stops with desktop publishing. Clients like this usually have the idea that multipage documents, an eight-page or 12-page newsletter for example, can be produced in final form in massive quantities with full color on a standard 8½" x 11" laser printer. They're usually shocked to learn that this kind of job can require use of a service bureau, that it means printing the work on a press, and that charges for these services are over and above those charged by the desktop publisher.

- Believing that the text they provide on disk — chock full of tabs, extra carriage returns and other awkward attempts to emulate complex formatting on some primitive printer — can be simply and instantly turned into beautiful camera-ready copy with no extra charge for fixing their mistakes.

## NICKEL-AND-DIMERS

Clients like this always find reasons for charges to be deducted from everything they're billed. Unlike clients who expect more than is promised, nickel and dimers often like the work you've done. They just don't like their final bill, even when they've received accurate estimates in advance. Usually, they also expect every little change to be made at no additional cost, even if the "little" change turns out to be major.

## TIME WASTERS

These clients eat into your profits with lengthy chats during every office visit. They want to discuss not only their project but the world situation, the nation's economy, local issues or, worse yet, draw you into lengthy debate on these or other matters.

## CHANGERS

These clients make changes with every proof, often rewriting extensively and making changes on a "final" proof that should have been caught in their initial editing and proofing. The result is that your "final" proof becomes five or six or seven or eight "final" proofs, with the client often expecting this to be covered in the price of the original estimate.

## TERMINOLOGY KNOWERS

You can be led astray by these clients; they have just enough knowledge of desktop publishing and printing terminology to get well into the start of a project. Then a suggestion for changes is made using terms of the trade and it's clear the client has no idea what you're talking about. Elyse Chapman of Claremont, California, says of this type of client, "They know terminology, but they really don't know what it means. They're smart enough to use it correctly but suddenly you've lost them. You can tell they're in a fog and don't know what you're talking about. You can get into a job and they'll come up with just a little bit of knowledge about it, yet they don't really understand all you're doing."

## CHEATS

Con artists are found in every kind of business and printing-related businesses are no exceptions, especially small operations. Desktop publishing's a relatively new industry and many people outside the business don't understand it yet. Maybe that's why so few desktop publishers report run-ins with outright cheats. Con artists have been around the printing business for years, though, and I suspect we'll see more of them as desktop publishing becomes more widely understood by the public and in business circles.

Sometimes these are outright scams, such as the man who comes around claiming to represent an organization that you've never heard of for the blind or deaf. He insists that since you made a contribution last year, you must make one again. Usually, he won't ask for much, $10 or $15 or $20. Multiply that by the number of businesses in a town and if even 10 percent are suckers, he's come away with a sizable chunk of cash. If others are present when you're hit up for the money, so much the better. He's not afraid to make a scene and he's confident you'll contribute since you don't want it to look to your associates or clients like you won't help a worthwhile organization.

Other times, the scams are less obvious. Clients will order large quantities of work with no intention of ever paying for it, for example. Dennis & Linny Stovall say they've had more trouble with the bookselling side of their business than they have on the service bureau side. For example, they've had wholesalers order thousands of dollars worth of books when the wholesalers knew they were going out of business. Just because this happened on the publishing side doesn't mean it can't or won't happen to them as desktop publishers. As society as a whole becomes more familiar with who desktop publishers are and what we do, we'll see more scams. This doesn't mean we should be paranoid — just careful. And not surprised.

## BIGOTRY, UNETHICAL AND ILLEGAL JOBS

Sometimes a person will bring a job in, offer to pay cash, and want the job back as soon as possible. It may contain racial slurs or inflammatory political innuendos or attacks on specific individuals. Sometimes the work clearly is illegal or unethical. Most of us would turn down such work but if you accept the cash you face a dilemma. Since you accepted the cash, you may be legally obligated to complete the project even if it's clearly illegal, unethical or bigoted.

The solution in this case is clear. Be sure that anyone involved in accepting work looks jobs over carefully before accepting them and knows how to tactfully refuse a job. Of course, the other out is that if the person bringing the work knows you'll go to the police, they may not make a fuss provided you refund their money. On the other hand, they could shoot you. It happens.

Of the seven types of problem clients outlined here, all but the last create situations that put pennies in your pockets for hours of time when the real goal is to keep business focused on earning enough profit to gain adequate returns on our investment of time, energy and capital. The latter type of client doesn't even do that, but simply wastes your time and puts no money in your pocket.

# No price too high

Most of us would draw the line at doing work that was bigoted, unethical or clearly illegal but beyond that, as Jim Dornbos of Saginaw, Michigan, points out, "Anybody's worth dealing with for the right price. For some of those people, the price is ridiculously high."

# Require contracts

Aside from pricing services higher for difficult clients, there are other ways to keep your profit margin on an even keel. One of the best is to have clearly written contracts that spell out precisely what is and is not included in an original estimate and any subsequent work, and to make sure that the client understands terms and conditions spelled out in the contract. Even a strict contract may not eliminate problems. "One of our worst clients," say the Stovalls, "was someone who we had under a strict contract." The Stovalls realized the man would be troublesome, so they drafted the strict contract to give him "fewer avenues to complain."

# Just say no

Another way to deal with difficult clients is to learn to "just say no" to jobs that look like trouble. The trick here is to do so tactfully. It may be that next time around, the person will bring a job that you really want to do.

## Client education

Yet another tack is client education. Sometimes a little goes a long way toward improving a working relationship that got off to a bad start. Any time I'm working with a new client, I start on the assumption that at some point clarification or explanation will be needed of why things need to be done a specific way, such as providing copy on disk unformatted. In past businesses, some of our best clients turned out to be those who caused the most grief in the early stages of the business relationship, but they were willing to listen and learn. Had I taken the approach that some desktop publishers use and written them off as clients because of unrealistic expectations the first time around, we'd have had far fewer clients.

At the same time, I have little tolerance for clients who come back time after time with unrealistic expectations, constant demands for numerous changes job after job, and especially for those who ask for major changes with every proof. The first time around, I work with the client, explain what's expected and point out why demands they are making will delay their work. The second time around, I'm less tolerant, though I still try to work with the client. By the third time the client ought to know better, so I've tightened up the contract as much as possible, specific information is provided about any delays caused by the client, and my fees reflect additional costs proportional to extra work being caused by this client.

## Be specific

We can hardly blame all problems on clients if we haven't explained exactly what we expect of them. One obvious way to do this is through a contract. Another is to provide clients with specific information beforehand. For example, if copy must be unformatted or saved in a specific word processing format, give the client a handout stating what's wanted. Let the client know if you don't want copy centered, underlined, tabbed, etc. Make it clear to the client both in writing and orally, at the time they're given this information, that failure to follow instructions will result in additional charges. If only black and white photos with good image quality are acceptable, let the client know in advance. Otherwise you may get color photos or black and white photos so muddy that you can't tell a cat from a catfish. Let the client know why halftones are necessary. Scanner technology may be great, but it's still not going to make a Mona Lisa out of photos with barely distinguishable features.

## Be patient and listen

Clients who come around and seem to be wasting our time sometimes are valuable resources. Often, they know others in the community who need similar work done and they can refer this work to you, though you may never know about the referral. Casual conversation is also a good way to pick up tips about other potential clients. Sometimes just a few words mentioned offhandedly are enough to tip you off to potential work, and the person making the remark may not even be aware of it. Of course, if you're on deadline for a major project and you really don't have time to talk, it's best to try a tactful out, "Gee, Joe. I'd love to talk with you some more but I've got to have this newsletter done by 3 o'clock because it's going on the press at four. Why don't you come see me at 1 o'clock Wednesday?"

You've let Joe know you're swamped with work right now but that you'd like to see him and, even better, you've offered Joe the option of an appointment so that you'll have time to talk.

## Draft a statement of business purpose

C.J. Metschke of The Monterey Press in Grayslake, Illinois, drafted a "purpose in business" statement. While it forced her to focus on business goals and objectives, a side benefit is that it helps her keep focused on the kinds of clients she wants. "It's as easy to get a good client as a bad client," she explains, "and it's easier to keep a good client. I find that when I focus on doing the best job I can for a client, everything else falls into place, including the money. That doesn't mean I ignore the money."

Metschke's "purpose in business" is "to establish a business that provides me and anyone who works with me an opportunity for personal and creative growth; to work on projects and with clients who are committed to excellence and who are making positive contributions to the world and whose work is in harmony with my purposes and values; and to realize significant financial compensation for my work efforts by providing high value to my clients."

Incidentally, Metschke points out that making a positive contribution to the world "doesn't have to be curing cancer," though she would not do work for a tobacco company or a furrier. "It helps if I'm enthusiastic about my client's project. These are the kinds of things that help keep me focused on the kind of work I really want to go after."

# Choose volunteer work carefully

Especially for those just beginning, pro bono work is one way to build business. For desktop publishers, though, it's easy to get involved in volunteer projects that eat up time, leaving little or no room for paying projects. Metschke had this experience with a not-for-profit organization. "I thought I was giving them a real value," she says. "They wanted cheap and only cheap so we had a lot of misunderstandings as far as what was being provided." Metschke got involved through a friend, but it "just grew and grew. I said I needed to start charging for my time. What I learned was that they were not valuing what I was giving them."

For the near future, Metschke says, she'll either write non-profit organizations a check or if she does volunteer work for them, it will be services unrelated to services she offers clients.

I had a similar experience with a worthwhile non-profit organization for which I'd volunteered to produce a newsletter. Total time on project should have been no more than twenty-five hours, spread over several weeks. Others involved did not meet deadlines, yet I was expected to complete this project on time even though my deadlines for paying projects were backing up and the holidays were fast approaching. I reached the point where I had sixty-seven hours into the project, at least twelve due to copy not arriving the way I needed it. I simply had to say enough is enough. When I wrapped things up, I was four days behind on other projects, but worse yet the ripple effect kicked in and a month later I was still trying to catch up on other commitments as a result of those four missed days.

Pro bono's a good way to get your name out to the public if you're not known and it can lead to additional business. Because of situations like those mentioned here, however, I don't recommend it as a sole source of building business, and it should be undertaken carefully.

# Some general guidelines

The real trick in dealing with difficult clients is knowing when to spend time with them and when not to. Experience is a good teacher here, and as we improve job and communications skills, we usually find it easier to work with clients. Other rules come into play as well, though.

### GO WITH YOUR GUT REACTION

"I've learned that when I don't follow my little voice right at the beginning, I'm in trouble," says Carol Pentleton.

### GO WITH THE FLOW

Any of us who plan to be in business for the long-haul needs to realize there are times when it pays to be flexible. "You have to learn to adapt, to go with the flow," says Elyse Chapman, who notes that satisfied clients keep you working. When Chapman encounters demanding customers, she looks for a way to "bow out of it gracefully so there's not an angry person running around town telling how you're difficult to work with."

## STAND YOUR GROUND

Just because a client demands price adjustments or makes a scene it's not necessary to give in. Some clients use these tactics with everyone in an effort to shave a few pennies or dollars off of their bills. Be firm about fees and charges when you're certain you can back them up.

## BE FAIR

If a client has a valid complaint, be fair and make appropriate adjustments, even if asking for the adjustment means going to a third party, like a printer.

## IF YOU MAKE A MISTAKE, GET ON WITH BUSINESS

All of us make mistakes. We're not exempt just because we're in business. We make business decisions every day. Even making no decision is a decision. Business decisions can be costly and sometimes they have unforeseen consequences far down the road from the time they are made. Dwelling on past decisions accomplishes nothing. The best we can do is learn from mistakes, weigh previous decisions in dealing with current business conditions, and get on with business.

# Walking the tightwire

At its best, dealing with difficult clients is a balancing act. A business with the right checks in place has a safety net in case of a fall. Business can, and often does, go on without the use of a safety net but it requires more skill and courage, and a willingness to pick yourself up and start over if you survive a plunge.

# Chapter 7

# All Factors Considered

As a new publisher in early 1984, I entered the business world with complete naiveté about the differences between running a business and maintaining a home budget. Like many new entrepreneurs, I wrongly assumed that managing a business required the same set of skills as running a household. It didn't take long to realize, however, that a business cannot operate on the assumption that the status quo is satisfactory. A business cannot afford to be static, and from the day you hang out a shingle, your business will enter a constant state of flux, for better or worse.

For most of us, this means one of our main goals is to see our business grow. For some businesses, growth comes rapidly, for others it comes slowly and steadily. Sometimes, it never comes. In any case, a business can reach a point where financing — say to acquire a vital piece of equipment — is a desirable option that allows you to hang onto more working capital. There are many financing options, including leases directly with vendors. Many vendors, however, are reluctant to lease to home-based businesses, and many banks and other financial institutions will not deal with startup operations or home-based businesses. If you happen to fall into both categories, you have two strikes against you before you even step up to the plate.

During the course of interviewing for this book, I found that few desktop publishers were aware of factoring, a sometimes viable and valuable financing option. Of the handful who knew what factoring was, only a couple had used it. Of those who understood factoring, most seemed to openly disdain it. I find this ironic for two reasons. First, anyone who has ever used a credit card has used a form of factoring. Secondly, for a new, relatively unestablished business, it can offer financing when no other options are available.

Factoring isn't for every situation, however. While accelerated growth is the main reason a company uses a factor, the factor may require that you have substantial receivables — say between $10,000 and $2 million a month. If your company is in its formative stages and you've started, as many of us have, on a shoestring with limited capital, and you're experiencing rapid growth, the cold reality is that you'll have to find other solutions to your need for working capital, starting with your own pocketbooks and those of family and friends — if you can convince them to lend you the money.

Of course, if your business can grow and prosper on an entirely cash on (or before) delivery basis, you may never need to do any financing, and factoring won't be a concern. In my experience, however, the smaller the community in which you do business, the more likely it is you will be expected to extend credit to your customers. In my neck of the world, and in every business I've owned, it was clear from the start that if we wanted to do business with business, we had to offer terms. If we didn't, no law said anyone had to do business with us, and many businesses would not have. At the same time, I've often been surprised by how many businesses, once they get to know you, offer payment at the close of a sale, before services are rendered. As David Hart of Commercial Factors puts it, "In today's economy a business has no alternative when it comes to extending terms. A business can't expect to collect on a COD basis. If a company wants to sell its product or service, it must accept the terms the customer has established."

Fortunately, today's software makes sophisticated billing available to even the smallest of businesses, thus there's no reason for clients or other businesses to know that we're a small or home-based company, unless we choose to tell them. This same software also makes it easier to improve cash flow by allowing a company to bill immediately upon completion of a job — an often tedious task with manual billing systems when even moderate amounts of receivables are involved. This means it's quite easy to offer customers the incentive of a discount for early payment or the penalty of interest on a late amount.

The balance of the information in this chapter is provided by, and used with permission of, Commercial Factors, 1609 W. Magnolia Blvd. Ste. A, Burbank, CA 91506, (800) 937-7887. It addresses cash flow, credit checking, factoring, and provides information about some common financing methods.

# Oh where, oh where has all the cash gone?

According to Commercial Factors of Burbank, Calif., a major problem facing small businesses today is lack of cash flow because money is tied up in accounts receivable and bad debt. Many young, growing companies, and even established ones, place the total emphasis on making the sale, sometimes at any cost. Many companies look at an order as money in the bank, which isn't true if it's not collected. When sales people are determining payment terms, the motivating force is not how good the account is but how to close the sale. Ironically, many times a customer is prepared to pay for products or services without any terms but when billing is offered, who's going to refuse it?

Many companies are afraid to ask for the money, feeling that it may upset the customer and the business will be lost. Once you get in the habit of letting the account go beyond the agreed term, it is difficult to change that habit, and most of the time others are getting paid while you're being put off because ABC Company is willing to wait.

There's an old saying that remains true today: The squeaky wheel gets the oil, and it simply means that the company that sets up a firm payment plan and sticks to it gets its money first.

Many companies extend credit to customers without even checking their credit, or if they do, they don't really know how to go about it. One of the typical ways a company goes about checking credit is to ask for references. So you check the references, and they say "Yes, they're a good pay."

While it may be true that this prospective customer pays this company on time, what about their other companies, and what is the amount of business they are doing with this company that you have checked out? Is the billing small compared to what your billing might be? Just because you get a good recommendation and your customer appears to be a good pay, that does not mean that you can extend unlimited terms. In fact, many times if a company is having a cash flow problem, it will tend to pay the smaller bills first and let the larger ones go.

A common misconception that creates serious problems for many companies has to do with extending terms for payment and what the real cost is. Most companies don't realize, or even know how, to compute the cost of extending terms.

For example, Company A was pleased because it had landed a big account and this would double its current billing. Company A won the bid by cutting corners and reducing its profit margin. The orders came in and the product was delivered. However, company A soon realized that Company B was a slow pay. Company B paid its bills, but payment was not received for 90 to 120 days. Company A, which was providing the product, figured that this was its biggest account and even if it had to wait for the money, it was better than losing the business.

Even though the company had doubled its business, it started to have severe problems, but before it was too late it sought the advice of an expert to find the problem. What the consultant found shocked the owners: the new business was not producing a profit. It was causing the company to lose money.

The more the company produced, the more it lost, and the underlying problem was simple. The company had to purchase all the raw material for the product, the production time was approximately 30 days, and after delivery, the company did not receive payment for an average of 100 days.

When the cost of the company carrying the terms was analyzed, it was found that it was more than the profit that was built in. Carrying terms costs money — whether you have a credit line, you're using company money, or you are using your own.

Another factor compounds the problem, and this may not be so obvious: what is the real cost when you consider additional profits lost because there is not enough cash flow to service new or existing accounts?

# Offering terms —
# where credit is due

In dealing with new customers, terms of payment should have nothing to do with the product or quality of service. The salesperson or company representative's sole responsibility should be to get the order based on the quote or the proposal. All credit arrangements should be made through the credit department. If credit is to be given, there are several things you should do to ensure that you receive your money and receive it as agreed.

The terms should be spelled out in the original agreement or contract, and by doing this you have a firm commitment and will be able to refer to it later, if needed.

Many companies, in an effort to increase cash flow, will offer incentives to encourage faster payment, typically a 2 to 3 percent discount if payment is made in a net 10–15 days. The problem with this is that companies don't always pay in the specified time, but they do take the discount even if they pay in a 30- or 45-day period. Your only options at this point are to either write off the discount, bill for the additional or add it to the next invoice. This creates a couple of problems.

First, your customers may feel that you're nitpicking by asking for the 2 or 3 percent. If you carry it over into the next billing, it creates additional accounting work. Another option is to discontinue the policy to those customers who abuse the privilege, but you may want to continue it for those who pay within the agreed time.

One of the most important procedures a company must establish is proper credit checking. Most companies cannot afford the sophisticated computer programs that give you instant credit information, but there are several ways you can do credit checking to insure that your customer can pay the bill.

There are credit checking companies that will provide information about your customer. It is important to shop for the best service and understand the agreement that you may have to sign. In some cases, the cost can be substantial and it may require a long-term contract. With these types of services, there are no guarantees and most of them have a disclaimer, so that they are protected in case of inaccurate information.

But there is another way. Do your own investigation. And one of the best sources for checking the customer's credit is by calling their bank. While a bank won't give out specific financial information, if the proper questions are asked you can get a picture of that company's condition.

Some questions that you might want to ask: What is the average balance in the company's account? The bank's response might be, "well, it's in the mid-five figures." By knowing the average in the account is approximately $50,000, credit extended to $5,000 may be appropriate, while credit of $100,000 would not be.

Does the company have a credit line or a loan arrangement with the bank? The type of loan is important. If it is unsecured it says much more about the customer than if it's secured. The length of time a customer has been with a bank is important. If the account is fairly new, there is no way to indicate the performance of that account. The other consideration is, "Why did the customer change banks in the first place?"

Ask if the customer is personally known by the representative to whom you are speaking. If the answer is no, it may indicate that the customer is not highly regarded.

Probably one of the most common practices used by businesses to check credit is to ask for trade references. The problem with this approach is that if a company is selecting a list for you to check, it will only provide companies that it knows have been receiving timely payments. It would be rare if someone would provide a trade reference and it would turn out to be negative. One way to overcome this problem is to ask how many creditors the company deals with, have the company provide you with a total list and then you choose the ones you want to call.

Another useful device is a lien search. This can be accomplished by searching the county clerk's records for Uniform Commercial Code filings (UCC). In Canada, you'll have to go to the Provincial Registries Office. This will show if there are any liens on a company's assets.

If a company has liens by creditors or by a government agency, you will certainly want to take that into consideration when determining credit terms. By following the suggestions provided, it will help you better control your accounts receivable and, in turn, will help your cash flow.

# A lending hand — maybe

When it comes to financing options, and which can best suit a company's needs, first you should be aware that bankers have a variety of financing options and each is designed to meet a specific requirement a business may have. The banking industry is continually implementing new programs that can best serve small businesses, but sometimes the business owner has a difficult time understanding why he or she doesn't qualify for a particular loan, and may even feel the bank is insensitive. This could not be further from the truth. There is nothing a bank would like to do more than to be able to give everyone the money that they need, but that's just not possible.

There are rules and regulations that a bank must follow that the general public is not aware of. So the next time you or your company is turned down for a loan, remember, your banker probably feels as bad about the situation as you do. But before you meet with a lender, it's wise to know what financing options are available.

## LINE OF CREDIT

This is probably the most common type of financing and the most desirable. The advantages are that funds are available immediately, interest is paid on the amount outstanding, and the interest rate is competitive.

## TIME LOAN

This is a fixed amount loan requiring no monthly payment. The payback is a lump sum at the end of the term, usually three to six months. The advantage of this type of financing is that you do not have any loan obligations until the lump sum is due. The obvious disadvantage is that you must come up with the entire amount — principal and interest — at one time. This type of loan requires a very good credit rating.

## INVENTORY LOAN

For this type of loan, inventory is used as collateral. Repayment of the loan is made as inventory is sold. The advantage is that funds are always available if there's inventory.

## ACCOUNTS RECEIVABLE FINANCING

This is a loan on a company's accounts receivable. The fee or interest is taken as the receivables are paid. The advantage is that a company can get cash for receivables that have not been paid. The banker institution will usually want additional assets, such as equipment, and a personal guarantee.

As you can see, there are a number of financing options available, so ask for your banker's help to determine what type of loan is best suited for you. They are trained to analyze a particular situation and recommend a program that fits your company's individual needs.

## FACTORING

The last financing option to be discussed is factoring of accounts receivable. There are misconceptions about factoring, such as it's a new form of financing, or that is only for companies that are in financial trouble. Neither is true.

Factoring is used more than all other forms of financing combined. When you consider that every time a credit card is used, a factoring transaction takes place, you can begin to realize the magnitude of factoring.

Using your credit card is consumer factoring, but it works exactly the same way as commercial factoring. When you use a credit card, the establishment accepting the card is really accepting a piece of paper in lieu of cash. If the business had to wait until customers paid their credit card bills, it would cause a severe cash flow problem. Fortunately, the system does not operate this way.

What happens is that the establishment sends the credit card slip the customer has signed to the credit card company. The credit card company then sends the money to the business long before the credit card customer pays his or her bill. The credit card company is not a non-profit organization, so it has to be paid for its cost in advancing the funds.

The credit card company takes a one-time fee from the total funds advanced. This is called a discount. The normal discount charge is 2 to 4 percent. That means that if a business sends $1,000 in credit slips to the credit card company, and assuming that the discount is 4 percent, the business would receive a total of $960 for the $1,000 in credit slips submitted.

Commercial factoring works the same way. A company that does business with another company and has accounts receivable is in a position to factor.

One of the first questions most people ask about factoring is how much does it cost. There's no question that if you look at factoring strictly from a cost standpoint, it is more expensive than the other forms of financing discussed. But when you consider what it can do for a business when it comes to the bottom line dollar, it may be the best financing method available. A company did a survey not too long ago and it asked, "If every one of your customers paid COD, what kind of a discount would you be willing to offer. Companies were willing to offer anywhere from 5 to 15 percent if they could get paid COD. The average came out to be 9.6 percent.

Factoring *is* doing business COD and the rates are much less than 9.6 percent. Factoring offers a lot more than just getting paid COD. Other services provided can reduce overhead, increase production, reduce bad debt and accelerate payment from customers.

Factoring differs from traditional lending in that when you factor, you do not borrow money, you make no monthly payments and you can receive funds in 24 hours or less. You control your cash flow by determining how much to factor and how often. You eliminate mailing costs and costs associated with collection efforts. You can spend more time directed to your business, rather than worrying about financial arrangements and collections.

## What factoring can do for a company

First, it improves a company's cash position. For example, instead of having $100,000 in paper, money is now in the bank ready to be used. Factoring also increases purchasing power, because when a company has cash flow it has options that were not available to it before, such as buying supplies. There are many times when a company can make a special purchase or take advantage of a quantity discount if the cash is available.

Factoring can even improve a company's credit rating. First, he increased cash flow shows a higher daily balance in the checking account. When you increase orders or pay on a more timely basis with suppliers, it gives your company a better rating. And with an increase in cash flow, a company can increase production and take on more business.

One of the services provided by most factors is complete accounts receivable maintenance. This gives the company a complete status report on all accounts. One of the most important services provided is the credit checking and evaluation. The factor will check or review credit for any of its client's customers. The factor will even check credit on customers that are not being factored.

The next step is to look at the types of businesses that would best be suited for factoring: companies that are growth-oriented, companies that cannot get adequate bank financing, companies with tax problems or liens, companies working through a bankruptcy, companies with a negative net worth, companies that are young.

You might be asking yourself "how can a factor help a company that has poor credit, tax problems, or a negative net worth?" The answer is what makes factoring unique. With any other type of financing, decisions are based on the strength of the companies borrowing the money. With factoring, the decision is based on the strength of the company's debtors and their ability to pay, and this is what sets factoring apart from all other types of financing.

## What to look for when you select a factorer

1. Make sure they will provide you with all the types of services discussed here. Some will not.

2. It is important that the factor has the financial strength to service your needs as you grow. Ask if they are backed by a major financial institution.

3. Many factors come into the marketplace, only to go out of business. Make sure the one you're dealing with has experience and stability. Check how long they have been in the business. A good indicator would be over 10 years.

4. Does the factor have offices nationwide to serve your business?

5. What is the factor's funding ability. Can they give you the increased credit line when you need it? If a factor has the ability to grow with your company, it should be able to fund up to $2 million a month.

6. Don't sign anything until a complete proposal is submitted. Why make a commitment until you have all the terms in writing?

7. Never pay an application or processing fee. Also, make sure there are no hidden charges in the agreement.

8. Be cautious if a factor quotes you a rate before having all the information about your company. Any factor that has a standard rate for all is not really providing individualized service. Look for a factor that has a program to fit your company's specific needs.

9. Ask for a client reference from the factor. This is the best way possible to determine how the factor services its clients. A representative or company literature can say or promise anything but the proof is in the performance.

10. A factor should not require you to factor all your accounts receivable. One of the advantages a company has is being able to control its own cash flow. By selecting the accounts you wish to factor your company can do just that.

11. Ask questions and expect answers. It's important to understand that factoring is really designed to help a business through transitional periods until a banking program is appropriate. That is why factors work hand in hand with a bank to help a business achieve its financial goals.

A bank realizes if it can offer a customer an alternative method of financing it helps keep the goodwill and other banking relationships, such as customer deposits.

# CHAPTER 8

# DOING THINGS BY DESIGN

B ooks about desktop publishing design techniques are a dime a dozen. Everyone, it seems, is a design expert who knows how to do it "the right way." Only trouble is, there is no "right way."

Guidelines devoted to the fundamentals offer a path we may choose to follow closely or loosely, but some stray far from the normal path. These strays lead us in new creative directions — or they simply take us on tangents that lead to bad design. The best design books lay a foundation of traditional printing and publishing principles, then add building blocks made up of the useful strays. The good-to-mediocre books tend to look only at either traditional methods or the building blocks, and the bad books focus totally on tangents that bring bad design. Unfortunately, the best way to separate the good from the bad is by reading the books forearmed with an already solid knowledge of typography, layout, halftones, color separations, screens, etc. Though not essential, a working knowledge of writing, editing and graphic design is helpful. The next best approach is reliance on respected review media.

Armed with this knowledge, books that focus on bad design can be filtered out and efforts concentrated on those of help.

Culling these bad books is important since there are enough theories about good design as it is. Many graphic artists tend to look solely at overall design and visual appeal, losing sight of what the flyer, brochure or book is trying to say. Many writers, on the other hand, consider only the written word and lock themselves into standard formats, failing to realize the importance other design elements play in getting their message across. A fortunate few can balance appealing graphics with the need to display text in a manner appropriate for the message. Regardless of which of these categories we fit in, as desktop publishers we need to realize there are other desktop publishers who are more comfortable in the other areas.

All of this might not be important, except that as desktop publishers we need to know what to say to clients who ask for an "unprofessional look" and how to find the right subcontractor or temporary help for a job when we have work overloads or we need someone with expertise different than our own.

# The good, the bad and the ugly

We've all seen examples of bad design done with desktop publishing: flyers that use dozens of fonts when two would do; overuse of photos, graphics and clip art when only one or two visual elements are needed; no focal point on a page for the eyes to zero in on; no allowance for white space. Worse yet, much of this bad design is coming from desktop publishers who are proud of their efforts and who are charging the same fees as those of us who emphasize quality in our work.

Opinions about what design options a client should be offered are about as varied as desktop publishers, but they fall into three broad categories: do what the client wants; go with the client's desires but follow sound design principles; or simply refuse to do poor design.

Not surprisingly, the first option tends to be used mainly by inexperienced desktop publishers and those without backgrounds in traditional printing and publishing. The latter approach tends to be used by experienced graphic artists and publications designers who aren't worried about having clients.

# Do what the client wants

We've all had or will have clients who've ask us for an "unprofessional" look. In some cases, it's an outright request. Usually what happens goes more like this: the client gives us a project and tells us to "do what you want but make it look good." So our creative juices flow, we choose one or two typefaces, and decide on our focal point for the page. If we've done a good job, when we're done we've used white space creatively and we have an attractive piece of work. Our client comes back, looks at the job and doesn't like it. From the client's perspective, the culprit usually is white space, though not always. It could be the client doesn't like the typeface, the focal point, or simply doesn't like the design.

Clients frequently view white space as the culprit because as far as they're concerned they're paying for the space so it should be brimming with type, photos and graphics.

This problem can arise even when need for white space is discussed thoroughly with a client in advance of accepting a job. It's compounded, though, if a desktop publisher has no handle on basics of design and printing. One desktop publisher interviewed obviously had no comprehension of printing and why it might be necessary to take a job to a printer. "It seems it would be common sense (to the client) that they're getting one good, fresh copy" that they can take to a photocopier, I was told by this desktop publisher. So much for high-resolution output, quality negatives, proper binding, paper selection under the guidance of someone who knows paper stock, etc. — all the things that go into making a quality product. To me, it's one thing to produce a job for a client and expect it to be photocopied because that's all that's needed. It borders on the unethical, though, to do so and charge the client a high rate when the desktop publisher simply hasn't taken the time to learn some necessary fundamentals about the craft and, especially, about the individual requirements of each client's job.

Every line of work has certain basics that must be mastered, and desktop publishing is no exception. For anyone who needs to learn the fundamentals, I highly recommend doing so at an employer's expense. Find a job at a newspaper or a magazine or a production studio that uses desktop publishing. You don't need to tell your employer that you plan to have your own desktop publishing business someday (in fact, it's probably not wise to do so). The job will provide a steady income, allow for learning at a more leisurely pace than is usually possible in self-employment situations, and provide formal or informal opportunities to learn more about day-to-day and long-range management of business.

Alternatively, many publishers and desktop publishers will accept interns. These positions seldom offer pay, but frequently provide excellent learning situations. It's even possible that the publisher for whom you intern may later hire you, i.e., become your client, since you will know more than other desktop publishers about their needs.

# Go with the client's desires but follow sound design

Several desktop publishers reported using a more "middle of the road" approach by offering what the client requested but only within the parameters of sound design principles. Rob Reynolds and Audrey Arntzen of Arntzen-Reynolds in South Lyon, Michigan, for example, do the best job that they can initially. "After that," says Rob, "when a client says I want to do this or that, we probably would just say, 'Well, they know what they want.' We take the approach that the client is right." In Claremont, California, Elyse Chapman of eec productions says "You've got to go with what's appropriate for the situation." What it boils down to, Chapman says, is the realization that, whether you like the finished job or hate it, if the client's happy you keep working. "The bottom line," she says, "is you've got to keep customers happy. If you don't keep them happy, they're not going to come back to you."

One out available to desktop publishers who use either of these approaches is used by Dennis and Linny Stovall of Blue Heron Publishing, Hillsboro, Oregon: "if we have a good contract and a good client, we always try to get our names" in the book or publication. "If it's a client we don't like, then we don't." Another is to charge more for bad design or difficult clients. Yet another is simply learning to say "no." "Being able to say 'no' is really important," says Dennis, "but it was difficult at first."

# Refuse to do bad design

Some desktop publishers have been doing graphic design or publication design for far longer than desktop publishing has been around. Others are simply confident of their skills and their ability to find clients. Many desktoppers in this category simply refuse to take on projects that involve bad design, viewing them as jobs that would make their businesses look bad. Among those who fit into this category:

Rick Ornberg, Ornberg & Associates, Des Plaines, Illinois: "I consider everything I produce an example of what I do. If the finished job can't be displayed on my bulletin board, I'm not happy with it. For an 'unprofessional' look, I may use Courier instead of Stone Serif, but the product still has to go through the same creative and electronic process."

Carol Pentleton, Carol Pentleton Design Advertising, Chepachet, Rhode Island: "I place a great deal of emphasis on design. As far as I am concerned, it's a total waste of time, effort and money to put together a piece that does not communicate as well visually as verbally. At this point in my career, I will not accept jobs from clients who want an unprofessional look. It would reflect badly upon me and damage my reputation in the field. I would go so far as to say that even 'beginners' should not accept that sort of assignment, as it limits the kinds of assignments you will be able to garner later."

## Making the choice

At some point, every desktop publisher must decide how much emphasis to place on design. Since design is largely subjective, the attention it receives will be based at least in part on market niche and personal, career and business goals.

My own preference falls somewhere between the "middle ground" approach and refusing to do bad design, but that won't be the right choice for all desktop publishers.

However, all desktop publishers must temper their decisions with an awareness of the hard economic realities in an industry whose technology is constantly and rapidly evolving. Kathleen Tinkel of Tinkel Design, Westport, Connecticut, sums it up best, "I've lost a lot of business as customers decide they can live with less quality. However, they later come back and expect rates to be lower" and work to be done "much faster than I do. You have to constantly be selling quality. If what you're selling is quality, then you have to be educating your clients to quality all the time."

Many clients, Tinkel notes, "have taken to looking at desktop publishers as keypunch operators" and consequently they have less respect for the skills that a desktop publisher needs. "Clients who used to have type set are now taking (the work) in house and doing it on a laser printer. They went from very expensive to cheaper to cheap."

# High-resolution vs. low: quality vs. quantity

Many clients seeking desktop publishing services clearly want quantity over quality, or at least they think they do. Worse yet, an amazing number actually think they're getting the same quality as before but at a much lower price. And even more view desktop publishing as something their secretaries can do without any formal training. Secretaries are expected to learn these skills in "spare time" or to know them intuitively because of adeptness at using other software.

It's often only after employers have tried this route and discovered their printed materials no longer look as sharp as they once did that they return to the desktop publisher seeking assistance, but by this point they've somehow convinced themselves (usually without bothering to ask anyone, and despite dissatisfaction with what they've done in house) that desktop publishing is cheap, quick and involves no specialized knowledge.

It's amazing to me how many clients see absolutely no difference between high-resolution (say 1000 dot per inch or better) and low-resolution (300 dpi) type on camera-ready copy — until they see it in print. Even more amazing, however, is that there are desktop publishers who consider 300 dpi suitable for any situation. If a job is to be printed on newsprint or other low-quality paper, certainly 300 dpi may be sufficient since the quality of higher resolution type will be lost in the printing process anyway. But do a client's job at 300 dpi on a coated or slick paper, such as used for magazines, and your client's likely to be the first to complain about the poor quality — even if she insisted that you use low-resolution because of lower costs.

## Ask the right questions

Dennis Stovall recommends interviewing prospective clients before taking them on, as well as learning to "just say no" to jobs from clients who seem like they'll be difficult. "Spend some time with the person," says Dennis. "Ask a lot of questions, find out whether they're headstrong, whether they want lots of advice but don't want to take it. Find out how cheap they are." He notes that often people who have lots of money are the cheapest, wanting to cut every corner they can. In my experience, they're also the ones who expect the highest quality of work, even after it's been explained that quality can't be achieved by taking shortcuts.

Types of information you might want to get:

☐   Get a rough idea of what kind of project the client has in mind.

☐ Learn as much as possible about the intended use of the project, i.e., audience and desired results.

☐ If possible, discuss budget, especially if the client is planning a repetitive project like a newsletter.

☐ When a prospect makes an appointment before coming in, ask that he or she bring along samples of similar projects that are suitable. This way it's easier to discuss budget and quality with a sense of the client's expectations. Paper samples, for instance, can give you a handle on the necessary resolution of type and graphics.

☐ Ask some basic questions to find out how well your clients understand the publishing process, i.e. what's the difference between a font and a typeface? What are their thoughts on use of white space? What results do they expect from desktop publishing? The answers will give you an idea of how much you must explain.

☐ If a potential client clearly has the terminology down, ask some questions that show a clear understanding of the process beyond simply knowing terms. This kind of question often can be asked as a hypothetical: "What would you do if..."

☐ Ask about the person's job and line of work, even if you know it well. If it's a management position, ask about management style. If the person's an employee acting on behalf of a company, ask questions that will help determine how much authority and decision-making responsibilities the person has. Learn who has final say on the project.

☐ Rephrase some of the questions you've asked to this point and put them again.

☐ Pick a job other than the one the client wants (one you've just done for another client if you're sure that client wouldn't object or maybe one of your own) and ask the client what he likes and doesn't like about it. Offer specific suggestions for doing the project differently and see how the person reacts.

☐ Ask questions to find out whether the person is locked into one idea or is open to looking at several designs.

☐ By now you'll have a pretty good idea of how easy or difficult this person is to work with. If you're willing to take on the project, try to refine it enough that you have some specific ideas and goals in mind. If you're not interested, try to find a tactful way to say "no." Something like "We wish you well with your project, Frank, but this just doesn't seem like the type of job for us" is better than just saying, "I'm sorry, we can't do this." (If the job's illegal or unethical, you may wish to use the latter.) Being on friendly terms with your competition can be a boon here, because if you know another desktop publisher who might be interested in the job you can make a referral. This will be remembered not only by the client but also by the competitor to whom you referred the work.

Depending on the type of project and its complexity, a good client interview can run anywhere from half an hour to a couple of hours — occasionally longer. It's time well spent if you expect to be dealing with this person regularly or if the job hanging in the balance is complex or long.

# Pushing for better results

Sometimes it makes sense to push clients for a better product than they're asking for. Often, clients make certain requests because of preconceived ideas of costs associated with desktop publishing or because someone else with basic knowledge of printing or desktop publishing told them it should be done that way. By asking questions, as Stovall suggests, we can get a handle on when it makes sense to nudge our clients into decisions that will give them a better result. Sometimes, differences in costs will be nominal; other times, costs may be substantially more. But if the result is a happier client, we're better off in the long run. Incidentally, note that I mentioned nudging the client into making a decision. Letting the client think he or she has made the decision almost always works better than forcing a client to accept your judgment, and if a client can be gently guided to that decision so much the better.

On the other hand, if a client obviously has a limited budget and some attractive designs are clearly outside that budget, it doesn't make a lot of sense to push. My own approach in such cases is to show clients the more attractive alternatives but not to press for them if they clearly cannot afford them. Showing the alternatives is important, however. I've seen many instances where such choices were presented and clients somehow found the money even though it wasn't budgeted. I've also seen situations in which alternatives were not shown, only to find out later that the client really had more money but didn't want to spend it.

# Sizing up your competitors

Many desktop publishers entered the profession with years of experience in traditional printing and publishing as graphic artists, journalists with extensive page and publication design experience, typesetters, book designers, technical writing, editing, or related freelance work. Others, however, entered the field simply because they saw it as an easy way to make money or it looked like a fun way to make a living — and it appeared anyone could do it.

No matter how we arrive in the business, it's unlikely any one of is truly a Jack or Jill of all trades. Each of us has skills we emphasize to customers, and there are aspects of projects that we would just as soon avoid — or should avoid. Knowing our strengths means being aware of our weaknesses. This also means knowing how much work we can really take on, even in our areas of expertise.

Not all desktop publishers need or want subcontractors but

most of us who are serious about our businesses will face times when we'd rather hire subcontractors than turn down business. The tricky part is finding subcontractors we're comfortable working with. It's another reason for staying on good terms with our competition.

By staying on friendly terms with competitors, it's easier to get to know their work and their styles of working. When you need a subcontractor, you'll know who to call on for the quality your job requires. You'll also know who bills themselves as a "desktop publisher" but doesn't have the technical skills or knowledge to do a good job. Or who excels at a skill in which you don't.

If you know your competitors well, you'll probably have a good idea of who to call when you need specific types of work. If the need for a formal interview arises, however, I suggest a format similar to that used for sizing up clients.

Remember, if developed properly, these relationships work both ways. Your competitors will know when to call on you when they're overworked or desire your exceptional talents.

# Independent contractors vs. hiring part-time employees

## INDEPENDENT CONTRACTORS

From a purely cost standpoint, there's no question that it's cheaper to pay an independent contractor than it is to hire a part-time employee. The drawback to using an independent contractor is that you have no control and if the person decides not to meet a deadline, you're up a creek. IRS regulations require that an independent contractor be free from direction and control by your business and that the person be established in his or her own. Some states have added further restrictions. In Washington, for example, as of January 1, 1992, an independent contractor must be filing a schedule of expenses with the IRS; have an account established with the Department of Revenue "and other appropriate state taxing agencies"; and be maintaining a separate set of records for his or her business.

From numerous conversations with others who have used independent contractors, it's clear that the IRS views its definition of independent contractors narrowly and will use almost any excuse to classify a person as an employee. For example, if you tell someone you expect them to spend 20 hours a week on a project, that likely will classify them as an employee in the eyes of the IRS even if you've given them no set time frame for completing the work. Theoretically, anyway, even if you simply set a deadline for completing a project by a certain date you could be considered an employer, since meeting a deadline could be interpreted as "direction and control" from your business.

In my business, I see no great benefit from requiring subcontractors to show evidence that they're meeting all these requirements and I see a lot of possible problems with it, including potential for creating an air of distrust when what we want to be doing is establishing relationships built on trust and dependability. So instead of requiring documentation, I simply provide subcontractors with a letter informing them of the requirements and their responsibilities and keep a dated copy of the letter for my records.

## TEMPORARY HELP

One way around the independent contractor dilemma is to hire temporary help, either directly or through a temporary services agency. The big drawbacks are that it's more expensive and you may not get qualified help, or you could get someone who knows the basics but doesn't know how to fine-tune a project for best results. Going through a temporary help agency can easily cost twice what you'd pay to hire the same help on the open job market, but a good agency should be able to screen job applicants to meet your requirements. Unfortunately, many don't or they don't do a good job of it. Perhaps, temporary agencies simply don't yet understand the needs of desktop publishers or why it's important to have a person who's already at a certain skill level.

On the other hand, if you've found a good temporary agency it may make sense to use it rather than going the independent contractor route. You still get the person for only as long as you need to complete the job and someone else still takes care of all taxes and other payroll deductions.

## Hiring part-time help

When it's important to have some measure of control over projects or when it's crucial that all deadlines be met, hiring part-time help makes the most sense. An ideal situation might be to find someone who only wanted to work occasionally and who you knew would be around all the time to be on call at a moment's notice. Sometimes a retiree can be found who's willing to step in on these terms. The big problem in desktop publishing is that it's such a new industry that there are few retirees around with appropriate expertise.

Most people seeking part-time work, however, are looking for steady hours and at least a reasonably stable income base. Many people, too, will accept part-time work while seeking permanent full-time employment. People will tell an employer anything if they're out of work and hungry, so it's not always possible to take a jobseeker's words at face value.

The big drawbacks to hiring part-time help are that you'll have to find something for the employee to do during slack hours or constantly be adjusting the employee's hours to fit current work needs (including laying off and re-hiring, if necessary) and that you could face a steady turnover of employees when what you really want is stability.

Be aware, too, that an employee demands a serious commitment on your part, and it may take considerable time and effort before total productivity increases enough to warrant the expense and generate a profit.

## Do it all yourself

Rather than face the unpleasant choices required with any of the other possibilities, some desktop publishers choose this option, realizing that it means working long hours into the night and shorting themselves on sleep on a regular basis. Some of us can do this without much effect on our psyche, others of us become grumpy and unbearable to be around after a only a short time under this kind of schedule.

Again, assess your own needs and limits and act accordingly. Within certain limits, being in business for yourself allows you to work the way you wish. You decide your hours. You can choose to work in the middle of the night or early in the morning if you're more productive then. You can work in bursts, if that's what feels right.

## OTHER ALTERNATIVES

Other hiring methods that may work for some desktop publishers or in some situations include hiring seasonal or occasional help and hiring by the project. Using either of these methods, extra help is hired as employee(s). However, it's clear from the time of hire that the work is either seasonal or strictly for the duration of the project.

# CHAPTER 9

# FOR YOUR PROTECTION

M any desktop publishers, especially smaller operations, like the idea of "working on a handshake." Indeed, that's the kind of image we like to project to our clients. For our own protection, though, it almost always pays to put in writing the terms and conditions of even simple projects. As with printing, the nature of desktop publishing makes it impossible to quote "standard" rates for every job that comes through the door. Nevertheless, any business needs standards it can follow to ensure that all clients are treated equally and fairly. Written guidelines for even small jobs provides that assurance, as well as a framework on which to build a business.

For example, if you have setup charges for creating a flyer or newsletter template, the client has a right to know them in advance. The same is true of fees for rush service, interest or finance charges, service bureau costs, et cetera. Clients also should be informed of, and shown if possible, the difference between 300 dpi printing and imagesetter output — especially if they're insisting that a quality job be done the cheapest way possible.

On longer projects, written contracts are the only way to go, offering not only documentation of what's included and excluded in the work but also accountability for all parties to the agreements. Additionally, a contract is a good guideline to fall back on if you get well into a project and suddenly find you can't remember details agreed to months earlier.

# Get it in writing

In some states, oral contracts are binding; however, it's difficult to prove terms agreed to in an oral contract, unless it's on tape. Putting agreements in writing offers more protection if legal action is necessary or if you're sued. Even in small claims court, without documented evidence of terms and conditions agreed upon, it's difficult to win a judgment. Legal matters aside, another reason for written agreements is that a job can go wrong. Even with the most sophisticated technology, problems can occur that are beyond the control of the desktop publisher. Written agreements offer the best proof that clients are aware of this.

Another consideration has to do with the trade practices of the other vendors we may use on a client's job. Among printers, especially in book publishing, it's standard to set "acceptable delivery" at plus or minus 10% of the quantity ordered, with the final price adjusted up or down accordingly. You surely don't want to surprise a client with a printing bill that's 10% greater than bid. Nor do you want to absorb the difference. Likewise, if your client needs a minimum number of copies, you must explain the need to order more — or pay more — as a guarantee.

# Proofs, agreements, contracts

## PROOFS

Most experienced desktop publishers require that clients sign a proofsheet at each stage of a job. Often, the job starts with a "galley" proof — type arranged in columns but otherwise unformatted. Clients who haven't been around desktop publishing or printing before often assume, when they're told the first proof is ready, that this galley proof is the final proof. In reality, it's an opportunity to catch typos and grammatical errors, do rewrites, and fix other problems early in the process. On the other hand, some clients who have been around printing and desktop publishing for years will abuse the process and insist on making major changes with every proof, including bluelines. A few even insist on press proofs.

A little client education, combined with proofsheets spelled out in plain English, goes a long way toward eliminating potential misunderstanding. I find it worth the time and effort to explain the proofing process to new clients and to make it clear how many proofs are included as part of the project and that additional proofs are provided at an extra charge. Most desktop publishers I know always charge extra for blueline and press proofs.

## AGREEMENTS

Many smaller projects don't need lengthy formal contracts, but it's still a good idea to outline in writing everything that's agreed to. Then if Mary comes back and claims that she was charged $200 more than the original estimate, it's easy to look back and see that the extra charge is because she made a major redesign after her flyer was finished or that she added process color. Written agreements complement but are not a substitute for proofsheets. Proofsheets give clients a look at the project as it's taking shape and in its final form; agreements can include estimates, specific details about a job, promised delivery date and any other pertinent information, such as what happens if copy is not provided on time.

## CONTRACTS

Information in formal contracts is much the same as that in agreements, but usually is more detailed. Contracts for long projects may include delivery dates for various stages of the job, provisions for fee payments upon completion of each stage of a job, penalty for late delivery of the project and other conditions.

With proofsheets and agreements, the desktop publisher usually sets the terms. However, projects that need formal contracts usually involve thousands of dollars. Each contract may therefore be different, since in it's often necessary to negotiate terms with each client, and what's important to one is not necessarily important to another — any more than what's important to one desktop publisher is important to another.

# Client responsibilities

By putting it in writing, clients shoulder some of the responsibility for seeing that the job comes out right. Too often I've seen profits eaten away by clients upset over a typographical error, a factual error, a misplaced headline, a dropped word or line, or some other major error. Though the client provided the copy and may have seen twenty proofs, invariably the argument follows these lines, "You should have caught this and fixed it. You're the professional, not me. It's your mistake. Why should I have to pay for this when you're the one who screwed up?" Rarely do clients look at it as if they've had twenty opportunities to catch the error and fix it. Even more rarely do such clients consider that desktop publishers often don't fix errors unless specifically instructed to do so because some clients insist on having their material prepared exactly as presented, errors and all.

Good proofsheets and agreements spell out clients' responsibilities in one or two simply worded sentences. For example:

---

### BASIC CLIENT SIGN-OFF FORM

_____ *(Client)* acknowledges by signature on this proof that all material has been reviewed and accepted except for changes as marked. Errors made by *Writer's Bloc* will be corrected at no charge. Client changes may be made at no charge on _____ (number of) proofs. Client errors or changes following the _____ proof will be billed at the hourly rate of _____.

---

Make a photocopy of the client's requested changes, attach the original to the proofsheet and use the photocopy as a working copy.

A good proofsheet (see sample, below) fits on one page, shows the date and time the proof is ready, has provisions for clients to accept work as presented, request changes, and indicate whether photos or artwork are provided and, if so, whether that material has been received. A brief explanation (one or two sentences) may be included regarding client delays in providing copy. Addi-

---

# PROOFSHEET

Proof ready: *(date)* _____ *(time)* _____

Proof must be returned by _____ to ensure delivery schedule of _____.

Type of proof: 1. ☐ galley   2. ☐ camera ready   3. ☐ other

1. A galley proof is raw typeset material derived from original customer copy; it is not in final form; the proof must be reviewed by the customer to ascertain correctness.
2. A camera-ready proof is camera/plate-production ready with no changes in copy.
3. Other proofs are defined as extraordinary — usually a third- or fourth-generation proof ordered by the customer at his/her expense. Such proofs are not encouraged due to the additional expense.

*Writer's Bloc* has ☐ has not ☐ received all photos or artwork.
If photos and artwork have not been received, additional production will be delayed until receipt of this material and additional expense or delay may be incurred.

☐ Proof OK as submitted.

☐ Proof OK as submitted but camera-ready proof is required.

☐ Proof OK with corrections as noted.

☐ Client alterations/changes to be made as noted. **This will result in additional charges based on current time and material prices.**

☐ Second proof wanted.

Customer signature required: _____

Proof returned to *Writer's Bloc* at _____ (AM/PM) on _____.

Please note: The attached proof is for your approval of types and sizes, and for checking of typographical or other errors only. It is not intended for complete rewrites or extensive additions or deletions to original copy. *Such changes will be charged at current Writer's Bloc hourly rates.* Please review the attached proof carefully, as we will not proceed with final work until the proof is returned and signed as appropriate.

**Make any and all changes on this proof, in legible writing.**
**Do not give only oral instructions.**

tionally, if more than one person is working on a project, checkboxes or initials can be used to show who did the last work.

# Marketing

Through naiveté or ignorance, some clients expect that a desktop publisher will provide marketing and public relations services at no additional charge. Those of us in the industry know that not all desktop publishers offer these additional services, but not all prospective clients are aware of this. Even among those of us who do offer these services, it's the rare person who will include them at the same cost.

# Help for self-publishers

Among the clients who use desktop publishers are a large number of self-publishers. Those new to publishing seldom understand what is entailed, and there's only so much counsel we can offer unless we have special expertise in the area. But there are a few basic and important pieces of information we can convey.

In addition to registering their copyrights, self-publishers will need an ISBN (International Standard Book Number) and LCC (Library of Congress Catalog) numbers for their books. Copyrights are the only registrations that are absolutely necessary. An LCC number is advised. The ISBN is used by bookstores and others to place orders for a book, and important if books will be sold through stores or to libraries.

Applications for an ISBN publisher prefix and a set of numbers are available from the ISBN U.S. Agency, R.R. Bowker Co., 121 Chanlon Rd., New Providence, NJ 07974. There's a $100 service charge that must accompany the completed application. How you complete the application determines how many numbers you'll be assigned.

Without getting too deeply into the machinations of the Agency, there are a several things to explain. The ISBN Agency wants to know how many books are scheduled for publication in the coming year, who the authors are, and other details. Frankly, this is none of their business, and a new publisher may not know how to respond. Savvy publishing consultants suggest that five to ten titles besides those actually planned be made up and listed. Doing so is no commitment to publish any of them — they will be publicized nowhere — but it keeps the agency from shunning the press and assigning too few numbers because it's small.

It is also suggested that the name of the publisher and the author be different. The reasons are similar. In neither case is the self-publisher doing anything illegal or unethical. These fictions simply expedite a process that should have no impediments.

Each title, or each edition of an existing title, is assigned a separate ISBN. Most small, new publishers will be assigned 100 numbers, all with the same unique publisher's prefix.

The Library of Congress Catalog number is used by some libraries when ordering books. Mostly, though, it is used by the Library of Congress, which will have a copy of each book on its shelves as soon as the publisher sends it. Getting a LCC number is as easy as writing the Library of Congress, Cataloging in Publication Division, Washington, DC 20540 and requesting the form "Request For Preassignment of Library of Congress Catalog Card Number." At the same time, the publisher should request the entire information and registration kit for CIP (Cataloging in Publication) data.

Copyrights are handled through a different Library of Congress office, and it would be a good idea for any desktop publisher to get a supply of the forms and information packets on copyright. It's all free, and clients will appreciate your concern and attention to detail. Write to the Register of Copyrights, Library of Congress, Washington, DC 20559.

One final registration should be mentioned, the Cataloging in Publication Division, mentioned above, is also responsible for producing the complex cataloging data that is on the copyright page of most books. Request information and forms from them, but be advised that they must see a draft of the book (in some cases, the table of contents and copyright galley are enough) before the catalogers do their thing. The value of CIP data is that it ensures consistent cataloging of a title by all libraries who might purchase it. Unfortunately, if the data is to be typeset in the book, it must be gotten early, and the Library has lately been running behind on this service. The alternative is to find an independent service or a librarian who can properly prepare "Publishers Cataloging in Publication Data."

# Protecting your business

An often overlooked area in which it can be crucial to get things in writing is organization of the business itself. This can be especially important in partnerships and in certain types of corporations. Even sole proprietors should have some information in writing regarding their business structure.

Partnerships and family-owned businesses are especially vulnerable to potential problems if there's nothing in writing. For starters, with nothing clearly spelled out conflicts can arise over who's in charge of specific duties. Job titles may help, but written job descriptions create clear divisions of duties. At the same time, it can pay to occasionally shift job responsibilities around. By doing this, a business may improve its odds of surviving loss of a key person through death or divorce. Potential for divorce is another reason to get things in writing. As a publisher, I saw situations in which one spouse controlled all finances and made all business decisions, a divorce occurred, and the other spouse was left with nothing.

The problem of losing an individual who is key to the business can be lessened through forethought and planning. Besides, the possibilities already mentioned, many businesses take out "key man" insurance on their principals. Blue Heron Publishing keeps policies on essential personnel, guaranteeing that the tragedy of death or serious accident will not force the company into bankruptcy.

# When to hire the legal beagles

Some attorneys would argue that any contract or agreement between a business and a client should be reviewed. Just like us, attorneys like to make money, and reviewing documents for potential legal loopholes is one way to make money. From a practical standpoint, though, it doesn't pay for a small business to hire an attorney to review every business agreement or contract. This is especially true for really small businesses — the one- or two-person operations, many startup and home-based businesses, and businesses that employ only a few people.

Still, there are times when it's wise to have an attorney review documents. When to do so depends in part on how much risk you are willing to take. One desktop publisher might be comfortable having an attorney review only contracts involving $25,000 or more; for another, the comfort level might be $5,000. Some desktop publishers may be comfortable never seeking legal advice. In any case, it's a safe bet that legal review probably won't pay unless a project's cost totals at least a few thousand dollars. An exception, of course, is if a document is clearly discriminatory or otherwise blatantly illegal.

Though he currently does not practice law, author Paul Edwards is an attorney. He suggests taking a course in business law through an extension program or community college. "Having done that, you will become well-versed in many of the [legal] issues" important to business, he says. "There are a lot of times when contracts are appropriate for all of us." Legal software can be beneficial, but Edwards cautions that the software often is written for particular circumstances and is not likely to be suitable for every situation. In addition, it may not be consistent with state law in all states. "Anything used along those lines should be reviewed by a lawyer," he says. "Be careful about taking a contract and swallowing it whole without reviewing it for your own situation. Some contracts are in the worst possible legal gobbledygook that will scare off clients."

# Rights and copyright

In addition to copyright issues addressed in Chapter 11, desktop publishers who are writers or who work with writers need to be aware of various rights and some practical copyright considerations.

## Rights

Under current copyright law, writers are considered to be selling one-time rights to their work, barring any specific agreement to the contrary in writing. Beginning writers often accept little or no payment just to see their byline in print; experienced writers rarely can afford to do so and usually pass up offers from magazines to "pay more when we can afford to do so." Writers must eat and pay bills just like everyone else; bylines don't pay the bills or put food on the table. Beginning writers who stick with it usually learn this lesson quickly, unless they have other sources of income to fend the wolves from the door. Beginning writers, by and large, also tend to be the ones who are unaware of how to sell rights to their writing.

For the desktop publisher, an awareness of rights to creative work can be important for many reasons. First, desktop publishers who are also writers need to know about rights not only for sales but also to protect their interests in any newsletters or other in-house or promotional material produced. Secondly, desktop publishers involved in either traditional publishing or who are working with self-publishers need to know about the various rights.

In the United States and Canada, the most frequently offered rights are probably First North American Serial Rights, which allows the publisher to buy first rights in both countries. Other rights include First Serial Rights (the right to publish an article for the first time in any periodical); One-time Rights (no guarantee that the buyer is the first to publish the work); Second Serial Rights (reprints); Foreign Serial Rights; Syndication Rights; Subsidiary Rights (which may be any other than first, but often refer to translations, audio, video, movie, or product rights); Dramatic, Television and Motion Picture Rights; and All Rights.

As a rule, experience writers shy away from offers to purchase All Rights. Some publications, however, only buy a writer's work if all rights are offered. In these situations, the writer must decide if sale of All Rights is worth it. When there is a limited market for the type of material being sought, it can be. In other cases, such as with a short story or novel that has potential for becoming a movie, sale of All Rights clearly is to the author's disadvantage.

Desktop publishers who offer consulting services to authors or self-publishers have an obligation, in my opinion, to be aware of the various rights and to guide clients to an awareness of their options. The final decision should rest with the author or self-publisher, based on the knowledge and resources provided by the consultant.

# Practical copyright concerns

In most books that address marketing of manuscripts and in most creative writing classes, authors are advised to place a copyright notice in the upper right-hand corner of the first page of their work, along with word count and rights being offered. Manuscripts are automatically copyrighted even if the copyright notice isn't there. The prevailing logic for including it is that it lets editors and publishers know you're aware of your rights. That's a powerful argument, in my opinion, but anyone who's tempted to include the copyright notice should be aware that some editors consider it unprofessional and the sign of an amateur writer. Their argument, also powerful, is that theft of copyrighted material or story ideas is rare.

I've often heard beginning, amateur or wannabe writers state that they submitted an idea to a magazine that then proceeded to "steal" that idea and put it into an article, or assign the story to a staff writer or another freelancer. More likely what happened is that the magazine staff already was working on a similar story, a staff writer came up with the idea on his or her own, or another freelancer submitted the same idea but did a better job of it or simply submitted the idea earlier. Though we each like to think our ideas are unique, it's rare for a writer to be the only one with a new story proposal. An editor's under no obligation to tell a writer any of these things, and most don't. Professionals accept the rejection slips and get on with the task of marketing another story. It doesn't pay to dwell on rejection.

While it's debatable whether to include a copyright notice on manuscripts, it's always a good idea to put a notice on newsletters, fliers or other in-house material produced to promote your business. Without the notice, someone could copy your work and claim "innocent infringement." A single notice on the work is sufficient to protect an entire publication, whether it's a brochure, pamphlet, booklet, flier, newsletter, or a self-published book.

The difference between simply including the copyright notice and getting the formal copyright registration with the Library of Congress is that in the former case, an infringement can only be stopped, and in the latter, damages can conceivably be won as well.

# Taxing situations

Nobody likes taxes. Well, maybe an IRS agent or a government employee whose wages are paid by taxes. But most of us don't. At the same time, taxes are an inevitable part of the American way of doing business.

As far as the IRS is concerned, if you gross more than $400 in a year's time from an enterprise, you're in business. It makes no difference to the IRS whether you're a legally and properly licensed business locally. Though this comes as a surprise to many people, an even bigger surprise to most is the importance of keeping accurate records even for a hobby, since the IRS can opt to review a hobby and, if it's found to be profitable, can decide that it's really a business and not a hobby.

In addition to paying federal taxes, businesses face a bevy of state and local taxes that vary from location to location. It's fair to say, though, that businesses often are dinged for an extra share of tax, licenses, and registrations because of widespread public perceptions, which carries over to state legislatures, that *all* businesses have deep pockets and are making huge profits off the public. Many businesses, meanwhile, operate on slim profit margins and when forced to shoulder too many of these burdens, no alternatives are left but to raise prices or close up shop. In a nation where small businesses are the mainstay of employment, but often the least able to jump through legal hoops, it's odd that they are treated virtually like the large corporations that can afford the legal counsel to allow them ways around the laws. But such inequities simply have to be dealt with — and planned for — if your desktop publishing business is to survive.

In some locales, it's also important to know the tax impacts of selling a business vs. closing up shop. For example, maybe you live in a location where the seller of a business is required to pay taxes due upon the sale of a business, and those taxes are based on the sale price of the business. Sale of the business at a hefty profit could mean a hefty tax bill in this situation. Or maybe you or your accountant claimed a tax credit that must be recaptured if the business is sold before a certain date. It's impossible to cover every possible tax situation, but it can pay to consult a tax expert or a financial consultant before deciding whether to sell or close a business.

# Choosing attorneys, CPAs and other professionals

It's easy to find an attorney, a CPA, a financial consultant and other professionals who we may need to consult from time to time. As easy as looking in the closest phone book in most cases. It's not so easy to find a professional who understands our particular needs, however, and even harder sometimes to find one who understands our needs and who we can work with. For many of us, frankly, the process of finding just the right attorney or CPA is a matter of trial and error and the search goes on until we strike the right combination.

This can be a long process since so many attorneys and CPAs in today's society are specialists, much like doctors have been for years. There are shortcuts to choosing the right advisers and one of the best, just as in the search for a doctor, is a personal referral by someone we trust. Then, it's important to schedule a meeting and ask questions about experience, specialties, length of time in business, and how they charge. With an attorney, for example, is there a charge for the first meeting and how does the firm bill? In our area, most attorneys bill in six minute increments at an hourly rate, but some charge flat fees and some work on a contingency basis in some situations. Even those that bill at an hourly rate have flat-fee minimums for certain types of work. Some charge for the first meeting, others do not. Also, does the attorney bill you if you tell a joke or engage in a little casual conversation during the course of conducting business? Again, some do and some don't. The only way to know these things for sure is to ask, and it can save money to ask ahead of time. Eliminating an attorney solely on the basis of a charge for a first meeting's not necessarily a wise move, but attorneys who bill on this basis offer some clue as to how they're likely to bill the rest of their time. If keeping expenses down is a consideration, it may pay to find another counselor.

If the professional has partners or associates, find out if you'll be dealing with the professional or others in the firm. There's nothing worse than scheduling a meeting with the person you think you'll be dealing with on a regular basis, only to find out on subsequent calls that you have to jump through a hierarchical chain of command just to get messages through. It also pays to find out as much as possible in the initial meeting about the potential adviser's style and personality. The sharpest attorney or CPA in the world is not going to be much help if you don't get along with each other.

Once the right combination of advisers is found, it pays to stick with them unless there's extremely good reason to change.

Reasons like death, your company or the adviser's moved, the adviser's client emphasis shifted, or the adviser's circumstances changed, resulting in a switch from working independently to working as an employee of a company. The latter, incidentally, doesn't automatically exclude an adviser from moonlighting as an independent; so before making a switch in this case, it pays to check out what effect the change will have on your needs. It may mean simply that calls will have to be made at night instead of during normal business hours. If that's acceptable, the business relationship can continue; if it's critical to have access to the adviser during daytime hours, it may be time for a change.

# CHAPTER 10

# MINDING YOUR P'S AND Q'S —
## THE DANGERS OF LIBEL

### A DISCLAIMER

*As much as we'd all like to think we're above reproach and that we always deal fairly with our clients, an unhappy or angry customer may not always view us that way and there are some real legal threats out there to trap the unwary. The information in the next two chapters isn't offered as legal advice and anyone facing problems in one of these areas should consult an attorney. Nor is it intended to scare anyone away from desktop publishing. It's simply presented as an alert to potentially costly legal realities that could face any of us at any time. The three areas most likely to cause trouble are libel, invasion of privacy and copyright.*

*While there are varying degrees of legal defenses against any of these issues, the best defense available to the desktop publisher is to be forearmed with knowledge of potential problems and to weigh certain business decisions accordingly, sometimes even if it means turning business away. There's an old saw that's often heard in newsrooms around the country, "When in doubt, leave it out." It means, simply, that one rarely goes wrong by being judicious and prudent in reporting what happened. As we'll see, desktop publishers would be well advised to use this same pragmatic approach in reviewing and working with material provided by clients.*

*In a book of this length it's impossible to address the complicated issues of libel, invasion of privacy and copyright in depth so they're viewed instead through an overview that offers the desktop publisher a resource for developing a basic working knowledge of these potential problem areas.*

# What is libel?

Before we can talk intelligently about consequences to a desktop publisher who is sued for libel, it's important to have a basic understanding of what libel is. Bruce W. Sanford, in his booklet *Synopsis of the Laws of Libel and the Right of Privacy,* defines libel as "a false statement printed or broadcast about a person which tends to bring that person into public hatred, contempt or ridicule or to injure him in his business or occupation."

Marshall Nelson, author of the libel and privacy section of *The Seattle Times Newsroom Legal Guidebook* and who is listed in *Best Lawyers in America* as one of the best attorneys in First Amendment law, puts it another way, "Any statement or inference, whether intended or not, which can be read as damaging to the personal or business reputation of its subject is potentially libelous."

An individual does not have to be identified by name in order to be libeled, nor is libel limited to individuals. Small groups can be libeled, and if an individual or group is clearly identifiable, whether named or not, a successful libel action can be brought. Nor is libel limited to the printed word. Other potentially libelous material include photographs, cartoons and caricatures.

Limited circulation or publication is not a defense against libel even though it may mitigate the amount of damages that may be awarded. Notes Nelson, "All the publication that's required for there to be libel is that the accusation be communicated to a third person. A person who puts a libel into circulation is equally liable with the person who said it."

In other words, say you publish a church bulletin that's distributed free of charge to five people. Your pastor shares the same name as a pastor who preaches down the road, and the other pastor spent time in jail for burglary. Your pastor, obviously, wants to clarify matters to the congregation and decides to do so through your newsletter. So in your article you meant to state that "pastor is not a crook and he did not spend five years in jail for burglary." But instead, in the editing process it comes out "pastor is a crook and he spent five years in jail for burglary."

Admittedly, this is an exaggerated example but errors such as this do occur, and when they do you've just opened the door to a libel suit regardless of how limited the circulation of the publication or whether or not you charged for it. Whether the error was unintentional makes no difference and you, as publisher, are the one who's liable.

Regardless of the technical rules of libel, Nelson says, "an awful lot of libel suits get brought because the subject is mad."

Trial lawyer Daniel J. Riviera of the Seattle law firm of Foster, Pepper & Shefelman agrees. "One who's the target of libel is usually really ticked about what's said." As a practical matter, Riviera notes, the target of an alleged libel generally has no medium to fight back. "An individual generally doesn't have a newspaper he can put out the next day to say 'this isn't true.' So the only recourse is a lawsuit."

In the event that a lawsuit is brought against you, one of the major defenses is truth. However, as both Nelson and Riviera point out, knowing that something is true and being able to prove it in court are two different matters. "When it comes time to prove it's true," says Nelson, "you have to be able to come up with live witnesses, willing witnesses and get the evidence together."

Says Riviera, "it's a lot easier to say it's true than to prove it's true. Depending on what is said, you might have to do a very involved investigation, both before you publish and when you're sued. More often than not, proving something is true depends on oral testimony. People's recollections on what was said can change. It can be very involved."

# The cost of libel

While truth is a major defense in a libel action, Nelson points out that it "costs an awful lot of money to win a libel suit." Not all the costs of defending such a lawsuit are measured strictly in dollars, however. In the early 1980s I went to work for two Alaska weeklies. Our publisher was responsible for operation of both newspapers and our editor for overseeing all editorial production of both publications. At the time I joined the staff, both publisher and editor were involved in a libel action that had been going on for some time. Both had to travel frequently to Anchorage to meet with attorneys and others. Consequently, other staffers sometimes had to tack additional tasks onto their regular workloads. If you have the misfortune of being named as a defendant in a libel action and you've never been involved in a lawsuit of any kind, one of the first things you learn is that as a defendant that you essentially have two choices. Your first is to hope that the plaintiff is reasonable and will be willing to resolve the problem out of court. Your second is that you go to court as the defendant. If the plaintiff is unwilling to settle out of court, the latter is your only option. If you're forced into court, it's best to hire an attorney who specializes in libel. Since this is a highly specialized area of law it gets expensive quickly.

My wife was forced to go to court a couple of years ago as a defendant in a civil matter involving a family trust. We tried to negotiate a reasonable settlement out of court but the plaintiffs would have none of that, even though the court ruling resulted in essentially the same terms that we offered. To date, our expenses for defending against this action are approaching $6,000. However, those expenses are a drop in the proverbial bucket compared to expenses that would be incurred in a libel action.

Anyone who has any doubts about that should ask Shirley McGreal of Summerville, South Carolina. Along with a dragnet of other people, she found herself smack in the middle of a libel suit over an innocent-sounding letter to the editor that she had written. The lawsuit was started in November of 1984, and finally dismissed by the courts in January of 1991. To date, her legal bills total a quarter of a million dollars and, although the libel action has been dismissed, her legal woes aren't over. She's now involved in a tortious interference claim in Florida over an innocent-sounding three-line letter, and her legal expenses continue to rise.

# A political tool?

McGreal says that libel is becoming a "political tool." Some attorneys would agree. "Libel suits are becoming more common as a political tool, and if a desktop publisher is involved in matters of some controversy, they might be hit with a lawsuit solely for the reason of driving them out of the dispute, and costs can be heavy," says Chad Milton, an attorney for Media/Professional Insurance, Inc. in Kansas City, Missouri. A practical consideration for those of use who are one- or two-person businesses, as many of us are, is who's going to mind the store while we're out if we're slapped with a libel suit?

# Your best protection

It should be obvious by now that, just as it is for journalists, a desktop publisher's best defense against libel is to avoid such a lawsuit in the first place. Says Riviera, "the aim is to avoid claims, not to try to figure out how to beat them."

When dealing with both libel and privacy law, says Nelson, an attorney with the Seattle law firm of Davis Wright Tremaine, "you're dealing with highly emotional issues. People sue because they're mad. Because of that, common sense about what is offensive to people will be one of the strongest legal advisers you have in the areas of libel and privacy." At the same time, Nelson cautions that "when you start getting into legal rules, your common sense can abandon you."

He warns that there is "no magic formula that a lawyer can create that will keep people from being offended" and adds that "if you make a person mad enough, they're going to sue." Nevertheless, there are steps a desktop publisher can take to reduce the risks.

## Indemnification clauses

If a desktop publisher literally is doing nothing more than printing or lasersetting a job for a client, Nelson says, "they may be all right." However, as a practical matter even in those situations, he recommends that the DTPer "always get the client to indemnify you. Part of the agreement from the person bringing the work to you should be that they will indemnify you from any claims against you arising out of material that they supply for the public." This won't prevent you from being sued, Nelson notes, but it gives you the right to go back to the original author and ask for indemnification. He adds, however, that "indemnification is only as good as the deep pockets of the person. The desktop publisher should be aware that if there are extremely risky things, you're likely to be sued right along with the person who brought the material to you."

## Disclaimers

Opinions vary about whether a desktop publisher should use a disclaimer similar to those used by newspapers, especially if the desktop publisher is acting strictly as an intermediary in the printing process. Some attorneys see no need for a disclaimer, unless you're a regular newspaper publisher with desktop publishing capabilities. Nelson and Riviera agree that a disclaimer is a good idea in a desktop publishing contract.

The disclaimers usually go something like this, "(Name of publication) reserves the right to refuse any material at any time for any reason without notice and without explanation." Some disclaimers also add that rates or prices are subject to change without notice at any time.

My own opinion about disclaimers, which admittedly dates back to my days as a newspaper publisher, is that they should be tactfully worked into any written agreement with a client, in small enough type that it's not offensive to the client yet large enough that it's still easily readable. While it may not offer a lot of added protection, it certainly can't hurt and most clients will not find such a clause offensive, especially if it's explained in terms that they can relate to their own business. The few times I've had to explain such a policy in the past, I've found that the best approach is to ask the client specific questions that you know will elicit responses that allow you to explain, in business terms the client will understand, why you have this policy.

# Constitutional protection

All publishers have a certain level of constitutional protection under the first amendment. However, within that protection, libel laws vary from state to state, so this cannot be relied on as a strong defense on its own.

# Beware the failing business and hidden plaintiffs

Both Riviera and Nelson urge caution when publishing anything about a struggling business. If a business is struggling, says Riviera, its owners "will blame you for all their problems. They'll be more inclined to file a libel suit than someone who just might shrug it off." Says Nelson, "if you get anything wrong about them, they will claim the published information was the basis for their failing. They have absolutely nothing to lose by suing you."

It's also wise to be on guard against the "hidden plaintiff." Nelson offers as an example a favorable restaurant review that comments that the new owners "really turned the place around." Guess who sued? The previous owner. "You have to watch out," he says, "for people who may not be named in a story but who will be able to convince a judge or jury that they can be identified in a story."

## Protecting your client

As a desktop publisher, you may find that some clients are offended if you tell them you cannot accept the work they have brought you because it is potentially libelous, or that it may involve invasion of privacy or copyright infringement (see next chapter for more about copyright). Riviera offers a suggestion that should satisfy their objections and which usually has worked for me in the past when I've dealt with such ticklish situations. The key is to point out to the client as tactfully as possible that he or she, as the publisher, is closer to liability than you are.

Riviera, whose firm has represented the Seattle *Post-Intelligencer* since the early 1920s, says this approach was used there with political ads that required the law firm's approval. "We would say to the advertiser, 'Look, we're in the newspaper business and we'll get sued, but you will too, because your name is on the ad.' In many cases we would say, 'Look, this is either going to be changed or we won't do it.'"

## Defending against libel

Let's assume for a moment that you've been meticulous about the work you've accepted from clients and that you've carefully screened all work for libel, invasion of privacy, and copyright infringement. Yet the worst has happened and you have been sued for libel.

At this point, one of your highest priorities should be finding a good libel defense lawyer (if you have libel insurance, your insurance company should help you out in this area). However, it's also important to remember, at this point, that there are legitimate defenses against libel. While any of them can be used on its own, often these defenses are used in combination.

As has already been mentioned several times in this chapter, your best defense against libel is truth. It's generally also considered a complete defense that will totally bar the plaintiff from recovering any damages. Other defenses that may be used include privilege, opinion or fair comment, consent, or reply.

# Truth

Since truth generally is a complete defense, Sanford's booklet notes, "the best safeguard against a libel suit is to make certain before publication that any potentially libelous statement is true and, even more important, can be proved true.

"It is often not enough to prove a substantially different kind of misconduct than charged in the defamatory statement, even though it is equally or more objectionable. Thus, it may be no defense to a published charge of burglary to offer proof that the person is a purse-snatcher. Likewise, if the defamatory charge is in the nature of persistent misconduct, proof of a single act of such misconduct is generally no defense; thus, a charge that a woman is a prostitute cannot be proved by showing that she was unchaste on one occasion."

Sanford also notes that use of qualifying phrases such as "it is alleged" or "it is rumored" are no defense against libel and Nelson observes that even among well-trained reporters there's often a failure to understand the "republication rule." Reporters are so well trained to always give attribution, Nelson says, that they can fall into the trap of thinking that if the source of the comment is identified, they're off the hook. "That's not the way it works. If you report that I said the mayor is accused of a crime and it's a false accusation, you're as liable as the person who made the statement."

# Privilege

Sanford defines a privileged communication as "one that would be libelous but for the occasion on which it was made." For example, under most state laws, statements made in judicial or legislative proceedings would be considered privileged. Nelson notes, however, that most of the time desktop publishers will not be able to rely on privilege as a defense. "The best rule of thumb is if a reasonable person would investigate further before publishing, you should probably check it out."

## Opinion and fair comment

An opinion cannot be false. As a result, Sanford states, "libel plaintiffs invariably try to persuade judges that the libelous remark was an assertion of fact. Conversely, the defendants in libel actions seek to have remarks categorized as opinion, for if they succeed, they will have two defenses among their arsenal: 1) a federal constitutional defense, and 2) a common law defense of fair comment. Nevertheless, Nelson cautions that "it used to be that you could be very comfortable with anything that was opinion. The U.S. Supreme Court has pulled way back from that." He notes that if the published material is "clearly humor or exaggeration, you're not going to be held liable for that. It may make people mad and you may have to defend against a lawsuit, but you're not liable if the reader would understand that it's not a statement of fact."

"Publishers shouldn't have cold feet about honest opinion," Nelson says, "but they should be very careful about publishing something that can be interpreted as a statement of fact."

## Other defenses

Those defenses we've looked at in this chapter are the most likely to be of use to desktop publishers. However, it's a good idea to be aware of the others, such as consent and the right of reply, and of "partial" defenses, such as retractions and corrections, that do not prevent complete recovery of damages and which are used in an effort to reduce the amount of money likely to be awarded in a trial. Definitions and detailed summaries of these other defenses can be found in Sanford's booklet.

# References

Two reference books that should be within ready reach of any desktop publisher and especially those of us who are also writers or editors are:

- the already mentioned *Synopsis of the Law of Libel and the Right of Privacy* by Bruce W. Sanford. Single copies are available through Media/Professional Insurance, Inc., Two Pershing Square Suite 800, 2300 Main St., Kansas City, MO 64108, phone (816) 471-6118; or contact the publisher, Pharos Books, 200 Park Ave., New York, NY 10166, phone (212) 692-3700; and

- *The Associated Press Stylebook and Libel Manual,* available from AP Newsfeatures, 50 Rockefeller Plaza, New York, NY 10020. For five or fewer copies, cost is $9.75 per copy plus $2.50 shipping and handling. For more than five copies, cost is $9.50 per copy plus $5 shipping and handling. Payment in full must accompany the order. The AP does not accept returns, so order only the number of copies needed. An added benefit of ordering this book is that you also get one of the two most widely used stylebooks in the country. The stylebook is rewritten and updated regularly and price adjustments are made from time to time. To verify price information, contact AP Newsfeatures at the address listed here or call (212) 621-1500.

# Insuring against libel

When it comes to libel insurance, there's good news and bad news for the desktop publisher. The good news is that it is available. The bad news is that it can be expensive and it may be difficult for some desktop publishers to obtain. All liability claims fall into three categories: bodily injury, property damage and personal injury. Most insurance agents or brokers will tell you that a business should have coverage for all three. My own approach, especially for home-based businesses that have few clients coming by the house, is a little more pragmatic. In my own business, for example, I have perhaps three to six clients a year at most who come by the house for any reason. Most of the time, it's just to drop something off on my porch or pick something up. In my wife's business, none of her clients stop by. Considering that most of those who do stop by are likely to have their own health insurance, it's difficult to justify the $600 a year plus in general liability premiums that we would shell out.

Libel insurance is another matter, however. Whether I work from home or at someone else's location, the potential for being slapped with a libel suit is always there. In my opinion, if as a desktop publisher you find that money is tight and you must choose between insurance coverages, libel insurance is the most important of the three. The odds that you may be sued for libel may be lower, but the risk you're taking is far greater and the costs and time associated with defending against a libel lawsuit could easily put many of us out of business in short order.

Further, there are only a handful of companies in the entire country that understand and are willing to write libel policies for the publishing industry. Fortunately, most of them are willing to write a policy for a desktop publisher. However, since so few companies offer this type of insurance, if you have no insurance and you are or have been sued for libel your chances of obtaining libel insurance are slim to none. If you are fortunate enough in that situation to have a policy offered, the premium is likely to be prohibitive. Theresa M. Coady, libel underwriter for Walterry Insurance Brokers, one of the largest libel insurance agencies in the United States, refers to personal injury liability as "injuries of the mind." In this category, which includes libel, Coady notes, "injuries are much harder to determine and as a result monetary damages are much more difficult to calculate."

A standard general liability policy, Coady says, covers all three categories but excludes "advertising, publishing, broadcasting or telecasting done by or for you. A desktop publisher may argue that they are not really in the publishing business. However, a court may decide otherwise and then it would be too late to obtain coverage. As a professional insurance agent, I would advise anyone remotely connected with the publishing industry to obtain personal injury coverage by either having the exclusion endorsed off the general liability policy or purchasing a libel insurance policy."

Coady notes that most insurance carriers do not have a broad knowledge of the publishing industry and therefore will not agree to delete the exclusion. "Then the purchase of a libel policy becomes a necessity."

Attorney Chad Milton of Media/Professional Insurance, Inc., another carrier of libel insurance, says "anybody who publishes anything is at risk for liability from the content of what they publish. Depending on what they publish, that risk can include libel or invasion of privacy. There's always a risk of copyright infringement."

In many cases, says Coady, the exposure of the publisher is minimal. However, it does exist. "It is easy to see that no matter how small a desktop publisher may be, the exposure is there. In fact, in many cases a small, one-person shop may create a larger exposure for the insurance company than a large, well-organized, well-researched business.

"Anything given to the public, whether through one of the desktop publisher's clients or as their own in-house promotional material, can contain information which would result in a personal injury lawsuit."

Milton raises the question of whether a desktop publisher who's acting strictly as an intermediary should be concerned. "Maybe, maybe not. You still have some responsibility for what you create." He notes that other situations can enter into the picture: your client has no money, goes out of business, starts to recant or a dispute arises over what was delivered to the customer. "In those situations, the desktop publisher might get caught holding the bag."

# Getting libel insurance

Fortunately, libel insurance is available to even home-based desktop publishers. Requirements include completing an application that asks questions about the operation, the desktop publisher's experience, and procedures for legal review of material for libelous content. In general, says Milton, the insurer requires some evidence of stability and professionalism, such as training. There is no specific criteria, he says, but an underwriter will look to see that the person in business for him- or herself has a reasonable understanding of the risks involved. Desktop publishers with several years of journalism experience, journalism training, or several years of experience in desktop publishing or a closely related field will get a better break than the person who has just bought a computer and "is trying to find a way to make some money with the idea of publishing a journal but without any experience at it."

Coady also notes that "the more experienced the publisher, and the more careful, the easier obtaining coverage becomes and rates will be lower." Coady also advises desktop publishers to look at expanding their libel policy to cover errors and omissions. "While the error and omissions exposure is not normally part of a libel policy, in many cases it can be endorsed onto it to provide full protection."

How does an error and omissions clause protect you? She offers the following example. "If a publisher is designing ads for clients, they may insert the wrong date, time, amount or phone number in the ad, causing a potential lawsuit. We had an example of an ad designed by a publisher for a massage parlor. The phone number was accidentally transposed. As a result, a private citizen had his phone number listed in an ad for a massage parlor. As you can imagine, that private citizen looked to the publisher for damages, and so did the advertiser who would be covered by the errors and omissions endorsement."

In some areas of business, being home-based can work against you. When it comes to libel insurance, that doesn't necessarily hold true. Rather than looking at the business' location, says

Milton, what the underwriter looks for is that "this is a person who understands what's going on and has some sensitivity to the risks in the content of publications."

# Paying your premiums

Obtaining libel insurance on your own can be expensive. The minimum premium at Media/Professional Insurance, Inc., for example, is $1,500 a year for a policy that would cover a small number of publications or a larger number of low-risk publications. "This is not like underwriting an automobile policy where you plug in a few vital statistics into a program and out pops a number. It's all judgmental." Consequently there are no precise premiums.

Coady, too, says minimum premiums can run as high as $1,500 to $2,500 annually. "While this seems out of line with, for instance, the general liability policy which may have a minimum of $250 to $500, it is because of the fear of the unknown by the insurance industry that the premiums for desktop publishers are so high."

Both Coady and Milton say group insurance offers a solution to the high premiums. "Individually there is not much one can do except pay the premiums," says Coady, "but collectively there are options. An association of desktop publishers could approach a firm such as ours with the idea of establishing a national program. If the numbers are large enough, it's conceivable that under a national program an insurance company may be willing to delete the publishing exclusion from the general liability policy for a premium as low as $100, giving the desktop publisher the coverage he needs at an extremely low price."

While group coverage may be obtainable through either Walterry Insurance Brokers or Media/Professional Insurance, Inc., a check with the National Association of Desktop Publishers at the end of 1991 showed no such coverage currently in place, though there was interest when the topic was broached.

Group libel insurance is available through the Newsletter Publishers Association for desktop publishers who are producing at least one newsletter on a regular basis. To obtain the group rate, one must be a member of the association. Membership fees are on a sliding scale, starting at $375 a year for a small publisher and rising with number of publications and a company's revenues. Fred Goss, association executive director, says a small publisher can expect to save $200 to $500 in annual premiums with the group libel insurance; for larger publishers, savings average between $1,200 and $1,500 a year. For more information, contact the NPA at 1401 Wilson Blvd., Suite 207, Arlington, VA. 22209, phone (703) 527-2333.

# Mind your own business — invasion of privacy

While the roots of libel law are grounded in common law that dates back centuries, Sanford notes that "invasion of privacy is a twentieth-century tort whose growth has undoubtedly been nurtured by a popular notion that Americans must shelter themselves from intrusions of the mass media into their private lives."

"If you say things about the private lives of people which are not public matters, you expose yourself to a lawsuit," says Riviera.

Sanford defines invasion of privacy as, "in simple terms, the right of a person to be 'let alone' to enjoy life as he or she sees fit, without his or her name, visage, or activities becoming public property, unless he or she waives or relinquishes this right." He adds that it is a personal right protecting the feelings and sensibilities of living persons only. Thus, "corporations and public institutions have no right of privacy, barring a statute to the contrary."

Yet while invasion of privacy is one of the easiest areas of press law to define, says Marshall Nelson, "it's one of the hardest to predict." The key test, he says, is whether what you published would be highly offensive to a reasonable person. The major defense is that what you published is newsworthy, that it's of legitimate interest to the public. "Whether judges admit it or not, they tend to balance the two sides of the equation."

Nelson notes that people tend to forget that they have no complaint of invasion of privacy if something is published about something done in public, as long as the published material isn't out of context.

Private citizens can become participants, willingly or otherwise, in legitimate news events and courts consistently have ruled in such cases that there is no invasion of privacy. For example, you're involved in a serious automobile accident in which there's a death. Although you weren't a willing participant in the accident, the event is clearly newsworthy and reporters and photographers at the scene are within their rights to go about gathering information they need to report on what happened. (Though you might be upset at the time the photos are taken, you could well end up thanking a photographer later if a claims adjuster wants photos of the accident).

# Photos and model releases

Nelson also cautions that when one gets into the area of privacy, the fact that a person is a public figure "makes it less possible to use their name for commercial purposes." If the person's name is being used solely for news or informational purposes, there's less likelihood of an invasion of privacy claim, he says. "But if you're using a person's name or likeness for a commercial purpose, such as in an advertisement or to endorse a product, at that point the person who's a public figure becomes more valuable."

It's not just public figures who are protected in this way. Every private citizen has this right. Says Nelson, "If a person is standing in front of someone's business, they may be in a public place. But if you're going to use the photo as an endorsement for that business, you'd better get the person's permission."

Though not absolutely necessary in all situations, the best approach that protects you is to get a written release from photo subjects for any photo used for any purpose. "If you don't have a release," says Nelson, "you would have to be able to go back and prove you had the person's permission to use the photo. If it's taken in a public place and not used in a false context, then you don't need permission unless it's for a commercial purpose. However, there have been messy lawsuits that have grown out of crowd shots, for example a picture that was used to illustrate articles that had no relationship to the crowd shot."

Called model releases, such forms can be simple (see sample form). In most cases, you can fit a model release onto half of an 8½" x 11" sheet of paper.

"What you're trying to accomplish," says Nelson, "is to get those photographed to sign something that says they consent to taking their picture and having it published. If you pay them money, even if it's just a dollar, and you cite that in the release, then it becomes a binding contract." Permission can be unilateral. "You either have to have a highly offensive document that

## PHOTO/MODEL RELEASE FORM

For value of .................. received, I grant permission to

.........................................................................................

its successors, licensees and assigns, to publish and copyright for all purposes, my name, pictures, and information concerning myself and/or my property photographed at

.........................................................................................

on the ........................... day(s) of .....................................

19 ...................................

Signature *(or name if subject is a minor)* ................................

Parent *(if subject is a minor)* ..................................................

Date ............................. Editor/Dept. ..............................

Photographer .........................................................................

grants permission to use the photo for any purpose, or you have a reasonable one that lays out what the purpose is going to be."

A good release will be dated, specify the period for which the use is covered, frequency of publication allowed and any restrictions that apply to use of the photo. Payment terms can be included in the release or contained in a separate written contract. Which option you choose probably will depend on complexity of your agreement with the signer. Warns Nelson, "no matter what a person signs, if your use of the photo is going to be extremely offensive," you're likely to get sued.

# Getting the release

It's easy to be aware that getting a model release is essential for sound business reasons, including protecting your own business interests. Getting that release, however, often is not so easy, especially if you live in a small town. Because of that, the temptation is there to shrug it off, thinking "I know this person. We've never had problems before. They won't sue."

In today's litigious society, that could prove an expensive approach. As publisher of a small weekly a few years back, I had some advertisers who frequently wanted photos taken of store employees or customers for use in their ads. As a regular reader of *Publishers Auxiliary* and *Editor & Publisher* at the time, I also knew of the increasing number of lawsuits being filed over invasion of privacy for use of such photos. Many of the lawsuits were originating in small towns, and sizable monetary judgments were being awarded by the courts.

To protect our own business interests we began requiring model releases for all photos to be used in any advertising. Many of our advertisers did not understand this policy, since it was a practice that had rarely, if ever, been used by the newspaper before. Some understood once we explained it to them. Others did not, taking the attitude that since we were the community newspaper we could take any photo we wanted at any time and do anything we wanted with it. As explained in the previous discussion, that's simply not the case.

# Defenses against invasion of privacy

As we've seen, truth is a defense in libel and defamation cases. It's not, when an invasion of privacy lawsuit is filed because, says Riviera, "the very concept is that you're telling something about me which is true, but it's private. So the fact that it's true is not a defense." He cites as an example a hypothetical ad about abortion. Included in the copy is the fact that an 11-year-old girl who lived down the street had an abortion. "This could very well be true, but it could very well be an invasion of her right of privacy because it's not a public matter. If the person is identifiable by the copy to a reasonable number of people, you've identified the individual regardless of whether you've included the name."

So what are the defenses? Most already have been presented here: consent (preferably written); and newsworthiness, with different criteria applied for public figures and private individuals. Another defense, one likely to be rarely used by most desktop publishers, is constitutional privilege similar to that discussed under the libel portion of this chapter.

As with libel, more detailed information about of invasion of privacy can be found in the reference books mentioned on page 132.

One final word in this chapter from attorney Dan Riviera: "I think that people do get the idea that big problems affect big business, that they don't affect me. That's not true. You're just as responsible as the *New York Times*" for guarding against such things as libel, invasion of privacy and copyright infringement."

# CHAPTER 11

# MINDING MORE P'S AND Q'S:
## COPYRIGHTS & WRONGS

While libel is potentially one of the most costly legal snares faced by the desktop publisher, a more common and also potentially costly threat that most of us are likely to face daily is copyright infringement.

As with libel, copyright law is not static. Changes occur frequently. The last major overhaul of U.S. copyright law took effect January 1, 1978. However, additional changes were made in 1980, 1984, 1986 and 1988.

Despite the frequent changes, though, attorneys Frederic M. Wilf and Bob Hughes say that with today's fast-paced and ever-changing technology, Congress has a hard time getting up to speed on copyright law. Both Wilf and Hughes are intellectual property attorneys. Wilf practices in Media, Pennsylvania; Hughes in Bellingham, Washington. Intellectual property law includes copyright, trademarks, patents, and trade secrets.

Copyright protection is soundly based in the United States Constitution and, Wilf says, "the drafters of the Constitution recognized that as the sciences and the arts changed, the statutes might need to change." Consequently Congress was given the right to change protection of these rights as it saw fit.

As technology has changed, says Wilf, so has Congress. "Technology does one thing and the law reacts eventually, if at all. Often it takes one or two attempts to revise the law before the law catches up."

Says Hughes, "Before computers came along, copyright law was a very specialized area. When computer programs came along, the patent profession was slow in catching on. Now there's kind of a mishmash of intellectual property law. Probably 10 percent of our work has to do with copyright law, but we must know it."

# Who owns the copyright, and for how long

## Today's law

Under current copyright law, a work is protected by copyright for the creator's lifetime plus 50 years, with a few exceptions such as an anonymous or pseudonymous work or a "work for hire." Anonymous and pseudonymous works and works for hire are granted protection for whichever is shorter: 100 years after creation or 75 years from date of publication.

"Work for hire" is defined in two provisions of the Copyright Act: Work done as a regular employee of a company, and commissioned work that is specifically called "work for hire" in writing at the time of the assignment. The employer or the commissioning party owns the copyright and is deemed the "author." The phrase "work-for-hire" or something close must be used in the written agreement. It's a good idea to watch for similar phrases. Hughes points out that "the status of a work being a 'work for hire' is automatic if the person is truly an employee. For certain speciality commission works (and this is rather narrowly defined in the copyright statute), you can make something 'work for hire,' provided there is a written agreement. However, for a large number of other works, you can't make it a 'work for hire' simply because you call it that."

Wilf notes that as a result of recent changes in the copyright law, there are now three basic assumptions:

- As soon as a work is created and saved in any tangible medium, it is protected by copyright. This includes pen and paper (even a reporter's notes), and magnetic tape such as used for tape recorders. He notes that if a work is spoken, it's not copyrighted unless a tape recorder is going, in which case the tape becomes a tangible medium. If work is on a computer screen only and unsaved, it is not protected by copyright because words on a screen aren't tangible and aren't necessarily something that's meant to be kept. Words become "tangible" when saved to a disk.

- Registration of copyright is now optional. The creator of a work does not need to register to protect rights. However, registration is a precondition to pursuing a copyright infringement case in court, so creators of copyrighted material that's potentially worth a lot of money may wish to spend the nominal $20 fee to register their material.

- Copyright notice is now optional. Initially, if the material was unpublished, no copyright notice was needed. Previously, if work was published without notice, five years was allowed to find and correct the problem. Eventually, however, when the U.S. joined the Berne Convention, the copyright standard followed by much of the world, Congress changed U.S. law so that no copyright notice is needed for works created after March 1, 1989. In the United States, a copyright notice consists of three parts:

- the word "copyright," the abbreviation "copr." or the
  © symbol;
- The year of first publication, if the work is published;
  and
- The name of the copyright owner.

In addition to the Berne Convention, there also are the Universal Copyright Convention (which isn't universal), from which we get the circled "c" (©), and the Pan Am Copyright Convention, from which we get "All Rights Reserved." Wilf recommends that desktop publishers use the circled "c" if it's available from their software; if it's not available, spell out the word "copyright" and use a "c" in parentheses.

Though a copyright notice no longer is needed, Hughes advises that it's still a good idea, "just as a warning that this work is subject to copyright law, penalties, etc." For writers or creators of other types of copyrighted works, it also lets editors and others know that you're aware of your rights. Incidentally, Hughes says, copyright covers a lot of things besides the printed word. For example, music, artistic representation on T-shirts, Cabbage Patch dolls, etc. Wilf also urges use of the copyright notice, even though it's not required. "In the case of litigation, if there's no notice, the violator can claim 'there was no notice, so I'm an innocent infringer.'"

## Previous copyright law

Prior to the revised copyright law that became effective in 1978, copyright law offered protection for an initial 28 years with a right to renew for an additional 28 years, for a total of 56 years (28+28 = 56). With adoption of the new law, works that already had been renewed received an additional 19 years of protection for a total of 75 years. Renewal is required for a work in its first 28-year period but upon renewal, it also gets another 47 years of protection (initial 28 years + 28-year renewal + 19-year automatic extension). Thus, a work published on December 31, 1977, for example, is covered by its initial copyright protection through 2005. It then can be renewed for an additional 47 years (28 years plus an automatic 19-year extension), offering protection through the year 2052.

# Do your homework
## Dig, dig, dig

If the only issues in copyright law that concerned desktop publishers were those discussed so far, things might be relatively easy — track down the author or copyright holder and get permission to use the material. But as we'll see later, areas such as public domain and clip art add to the DTPers need for awareness of copyright.

Before we get to that point, though, I want to focus for a moment on tracking down copyright ownership. While I was doing research for this book, the copyright issue came up on several CompuServe forums, including the desktop publishing, work from home, and MIDI forums. Most of the questions regarded exactly what we've been talking about in this chapter so far — how long does a copyright last? In the course of responding to one of these questions, the comment was made to me that it can be difficult to track down the owner of a copyright.

The person was right, of course, but if you want to quote from copyrighted material, it's still your responsibility to obtain the proper permissions. Nobody said it's always easy. If you wish to quote from a book, the best way to start is by contacting the publisher. For books, in most cases the publisher's name and location are listed on the copyright page, just after the title page. For magazines or newspapers, your best bet is to start with the managing editor. If the managing editor is not the right person to contact, your request will be referred to the appropriate person. In the case of larger publications, the editor's secretary or receptionist often knows where your request should be directed.

Things get a little tougher if a publication has gone out of business and you wish to quote from an article. For one thing, if the publication holds the copyright, that copyright is still good even though the publication has folded. That means you'll need to track down the publisher to get permission. If the author holds the copyright, you need permission directly and without a publisher to call, an author can be more difficult to find.

A good place to start would be to check with the Library of Congress. If the copyright has been registered, you should be able to get some basic information from material that is a matter of public record. Also, though writers tend to be solitary while working, they're a basically friendly lot so it can pay to ask around among other writers, through writers conferences, and on various electronic databases such as CompuServe, GEnie, Prodigy, America On Line, etc. Chances are someone, somewhere will know the person you want to reach and how to do so. Public and university libraries also are good resources, and while you might not get the needed information directly, you sometimes can get enough of a lead that you can track down additional information.

Since copyright notice is not needed on works created after March 1, 1989, the only way one can be 100 percent certain in today's world that you are not violating a copyright is to get permission from the creator of the work — even if you just want to quote from a message left on an electronic bulletin board.

# Public domain

There are two ways material can enter the public domain. One, rarely used, is for the creator of the copyrighted material to place it there. The other is that the material automatically enters public domain once the copyright expires. As we've seen, this can be a long time. The area of public domain falls under duration of copyright, Hughes notes, Under U.S. law, he says, if the copyrighted work was published more than 56 years before January 1, 1978, it automatically enters the public domain.

Even with work that's in the public domain, however, there is a catch: while the copyright on the work itself has expired and thus the original work is open to use by anyone, a present-day publisher can copyright a specific arrangement of a work. That's why, for example, you'll often see copyright notices on arrangements by Mozart or Bach and on church hymns that have been around for centuries. Wilf notes, too, that people often confuse publication with public domain. Contrary to popular perception, an article or book does not enter public domain just because it's been published and widely circulated.

# Clip art

Both Hughes and Wilf warn against using clip art for wide distribution or commercial use without first knowing what the licensing provisions are. "If the person distributing the clip art has properly phrased their work," says Hughes, "there will be a provision that allows use of the art for individual home use but prevents multiple uses, such as making 10,000 copies for distribution through K-Mart."

In an article for *WUGNET Windows Journal* in 1990, Wilf writes, "Clip art is not much different from icons and wallpaper. If you use CorelDRAW to copy an icon from a commercial package and place it in a newsletter that you intend to distribute, the owner of the commercial package is likely to sue you as soon as it finds out."

Hughes observes that without any stipulations, such as a licensing agreement, "there clearly is an implied license. On the other hand, you would not have the right to put the information in your own book. If you're going to use it in a book, it would behoove the author (desktop publisher, graphic artist) to get permission to use it." The same goes for using the material in a newsletter or fliers.

"The safest thing to do," says Hughes, is to contact the copyright owner and get permission *in writing*, for example through a confirming letter, to use the material."

Personally, while I understand Hughes' and Wilf's comments regarding use of clip art, I find it a bit odd that a clip art company would take this approach, especially since so many clip art packagers openly encourage their purchasers to use the material in their own newsletters, fliers, and similar publications. The whole intent of clip art, when it first originated for use in magazines and newspapers, was to give publishers ready and quick access to line art for use in their publications, often for advertisements. Of course, the publisher was expected to pay a fee for the right to use that material. Continued payment of the fee brought new clip art on a regular basis, and before long the publisher had built up a sizable repertoire of material that could be used. Nevertheless, check the rights granted before using anything created by someone else. Better yet, check those rights before you buy.

# Hide and seek, copyright style

By now it should be obvious that there are all sorts of hidden copyright traps lurking out there, waiting to snare the unwary desktop publisher. When doing our own work, such as in-house fliers or brochures, most of us are sharp enough to recognize when permission is needed. The real danger presents itself when we have clients, and most of us get them, who bring us something they've photocopied or that they want lifted from a magazine or book or even from an electronic bulletin board.

Many of these clients are either unaware of copyright law, or they shrug it off as insignificant. For example, I was told in a social setting a few years ago, by someone who should have known better, that it was OK to photocopy some obviously copyrighted material for distribution to several people "because attorneys have better things to do with their time than to pursue copyright infringement." Obviously, this person did not know that writers and other creators of copyrighted material are more aware than ever of their rights and he also obviously did not realize that we have at least one attorney here in our small city who does work in this area.

With today's photocopiers and electronic and computer technology, copies often reproduce better than originals and if there's no copyright notice on the work, the desktop publisher may scan the material without giving it a second thought.

Hold it! Wait a second. Maybe we'd better give it a second thought.

As we've seen, chances are good that the material is protected by copyright. If the client wants us to reproduce and distribute a Garfield or Snoopy cartoon, we're going to know it's copyrighted and registered and our red flag should go up. But even if it's work by a local graphic artist or author, we should be on guard. Of course, if the work is created by the person who's wanting us to do the desktop publishing, then we're on safe ground, since we're simply doing the job and returning the material for distribution as the client sees fit.

"Today's technology makes it much easier to copy material," says Wilf, "so the desktop publisher has to be more careful." At the very least, he says, a client should be informed that there's a risk of being sued for copyright infringement. "You also have the right to simply refuse to print it."

We want to please our clients, and some can get huffy if we refuse their work, even if we've explained that it's because of potential legal problems. As Wilf points out, a lot of copyright infringement is done on a small scale and, because of the costs of pursuing a case through the courts, "it becomes more of a moral than a legal issue, because nobody's going to sue a person who makes a single copy of a Garfield cartoon or a local publication with a circulation of ten." However, copying without permission anything with a monetary value, such as a brochure, musical scores, etc., leaves the door open to a lawsuit, and Wilf says he has seen cases where infringement cases have been brought even with small-circulation publications because of the value of the copyrighted material.

From a practical standpoint, Wilf notes, the small desktop publisher has several choices: you can have a policy that you accept no copyrighted material because it's an infringement; you can say something to your client (or not) and do the job anyway, realizing that you are running some risk but taking into account how likely it is that the copyright holder will sue; or you can inform your client that you will do the job but only after the client grants you indemnification. Even then, Wilf says, the desktop publisher "is always open to an infringement suit." As with libel, indemnification is not going to offer you much protection if the other person has no money, can't be found or, in the case of a business, has gone out of business.

Further, Wilf notes, "if you know it's illegal, it's illegal. The fact that it's only a small number of copies makes no difference." Nevertheless, he says, "if you didn't know, you didn't know" and that, he says, can be a good defense for a desktop publisher.

Wilf cites as an example a desktop publisher — let's call her Jenny. Jenny produces brochures and newsletters for clients. Bob brings her a newsletter and asks her to publish it. She does so, and he sells each issue for $1,000 a copy because the newsletter contains valuable information for his limited market. It turns out that Bob has stolen a copyrighted article from George, who sues both Bob and Jenny. "Jenny says, 'Hey, I didn't know because I had no copyright notice.' Jenny will be out of the case. Bob knew and should have known, so he'll still be involved in the lawsuit." Now another person, Jim, has a different, but equally valuable newsletter. Jim's newsletter also sells for $1,000 a copy, and he asks Jenny to publish 100 copies. He has a Garfield cartoon. Jenny knows it's illegal to copy this cartoon. "She could say to Jim, 'I'll publish this and run the risk of getting sued,' or she could get an indemnification clause, or she could refuse to publish it until Jim gets written permission." Under the law, Wilf adds, permission doesn't have to be written, but it's recommended. However, because Jenny had the copyright notice in front of her, she had actual knowledge of the copyright and therefore she should know that publication is an infringement.

Wilf notes that there isn't any single answer when the issue of copyright infringement arises. For example, Bob comes back to Jenny and says, "Hey, George isn't going to sue me any more. Here, publish this." Again, Jenny's unaware of any copyright infringement so she publishes the material Bob brought. This time, she's not sued but she gets a letter from George's attorney saying "Hey, you did it again. Cease and desist." Jenny again is on notice, and this time she's lost any immunity for any future publication of George's copyrighted material.

There's another common pitfall, says Hughes, that shows up when work is subcontracted to others, such as writers or graphic artists. "There's a common conception that because you paid for the work, you own it. However, you don't own the copyright unless you negotiated specifically for it." If a writer subcontracts work to a graphic artist, for example, the writer cannot assume that he or she can use that artwork for any purpose other than that for which it originally was intended. "To use the work for other purposes requires the express consent of the creator (in this case the graphic artist) and, if the graphic artist is sharp, he or she is going to want additional payment."

# Other red flags
## The hidden copyright

Articles, columns, short stories or similar works that have been published in magazines, newspapers or other periodicals may be registered separately as a "contribution to a collective work."

"Under the present copyright statute," says the Copyright Office, "the copyright in a separate contribution to a published collective work such as a periodical is distinct from the copyright in the collective work as a whole. In the absence of an express transfer from the author of the individual article, the copyright owner in the collective work is presumed to have acquired only the privilege of using the contribution in the collective work and in subsequent revisions and later editions of the collective work.

"As is the case with all published works, a contribution, such as a pictorial or graphic work, to a collective work may appear with its own notice of copyright. However, the law does provide that a single notice covering the collective work as a whole can defeat a defense of 'innocent infringement.'" In other words, a single copyright notice in a magazine is sufficient warning that none of the material may be copied without permission but if you want to quote from an article you may need to get permission not only from the publication but also from the author unless a work-for-hire agreement was in force. And even if the publication does not include a copyright notice, the creator's work still is copyrighted and may be registered, thus still requiring permission to use the material.

As a practical matter, authors often allow publishers to grant such permission on their behalf, but such permission is not automatic. It often depends in part on how much material you want to use. If you wish to quote just a sentence or paragraph or two, you're more likely to obtain permission to quote without payment of a fee than if you want to reprint a whole article, in which case payment is going to be expected.

## Ideas and titles

Titles cannot be copyrighted, nor can ideas and facts — only your expressions of them. For example, says Hughes, "one person can write an article about the steps in building a bookshelf by cutting 2x4's to certain lengths, et cetera. Another party could read that article, comprehend what was done, and then write his own independent article about how to build that same bookshelf. Provided the person wrote the article independently and didn't copy the illustrations, et cetera, that would in all likelihood not be copyright infringement." Hughes cautions, however, that "it is a little more complex than that, particularly where you get into such things as the plot of a story, where the sequence of events is itself considered copyrightable subject matter."

Hughes notes, too, that a distinction needs to be made between independent creation or development of similar works and outright copying. "If two people in different locations come up with almost identical stories, there is no infringement. However, if one of the two has copied the work of the other, that's copyright infringement." While only expression of an idea can be covered by copyright, Hughes points out that an idea may be covered by patent, trademark, and trade secret laws.

There are lots of tests to determine what's an idea and what's an expression, Wilf says. One of the most common is a two-part test. In the first part, a list is made of all elements that match and all that don't. The second part of the test considers the work as a whole. If there's infringement under both parts of the test, then there's copyright infringement. There's no infringement if either part of the test failed.

# Co-authorship

Hughes says a red flag should go up any time co-authorship is involved. "With joint works, each author, artist or creator is a joint owner of the work. Any one of the joint owners can publish, license or copy the work without the permission of the other co-authors, except that each joint owner is responsible for accounting to the other person."

Circumstances can arise under co-authorships, Hughes notes, where people cannot agree "and then it becomes a substantial obstacle to one of the parties trying to carry the project on without the cooperation of the other." Consequently, he says, any time authors, artists or graphic artists get involved in any co-authorship, they should have a carefully drawn agreement. "It can be simple, but it should have a carefully drawn arbitration clause."

He advises consulting an attorney with expertise in this area of law rather than a generalist because "generally, attorneys may not be cognizant of where underlying problems can arise." For example, a desktop publisher hires an ad agency to do some work and the agency in turn subcontracts some of the work to an independent artist. Since under the Work for Hire Doctrine the artist is not an employee of the ad agency, there's a responsibility to get written assignment of the artist's copyright interest. "As soon as you start getting other people involved in the work, have a firm idea of agreements.

"An agreement needs to specify who created the work. As a practical matter, I think most people don't do it. However, if the work's of any significance, you should get an agreement that stipulates that the person offering the work will track down who created it, if they didn't."

## Aside from obvious infringements

Beyond obvious copyright infringement, says Hughes, potential legal problems are directly proportional to exposure of the work. When a work involves other people or derives material from other sources, *it's a good idea to cover your bases in writing and document all dates, notes, whom you talked with, interviewed, etc.* Keep this material for several years beyond when *you* think you need it.

# Beyond copyright

Aside from copyright law, Hughes urges that desktop publishers:

- be careful about getting confidential ideas from other people (i.e., appropriating an idea for a book);
- be careful about under which conditions you take proprietary ideas (i.e., someone tells you about a story or book they think you should write, because you're a writer and they're not);
- realize that while titles are not copyrightable, they may be protected under law that covers misappropriating values of another and false destination of origin;
- don't rely on a sense of "what's fair" as a means of avoiding legal problems. In some areas of law, a sense of fair play may not be a bad guide, but "in areas of law where there are technical violations, doing what appears to be the fair thing can lead to disaster. For example, in misappropriating the work of another, quite often your 'sense of smell' may be a good guide." However, "in terms of complying with certain technicalities of the copyright law, simply doing what you think is

right and flying by the seat of your pants can cause problems."

# Registering your copyright

As mentioned earlier, to obtain copyright registration forms, contact:

> Register of Copyrights
> Copyright Office
> Library of Congress
> Washington, DC 20559
> or call (202) 479-0700

You also may wish to request a complete schedule of copyright fees.

These forms may be photocopied, so when you receive them make several copies and keep the original as a master. Your photocopied forms must be clear, legible and on a good grade of 8 ½" x 11" white paper suitable for automatic feeding through a photocopier. Forms should be printed, preferably in black ink, so that when you turn the top page over the top of page 2 is directly behind the top of page 1.

Registration costs $20 for forms TX or SE (to register a group of works); request schedule SE/Group if registering a serial publication. Cost to register serial publications is $10 per issue, and several restrictions apply.

The Copyright Office receives about 700,000 applications annually, so you won't receive an acknowledgment that your application has been received. Within 16 weeks of submission, however, you should receive a certificate of registration or a letter or phone call from the Copyright Office if more information is needed. If your application cannot be accepted, you should receive a letter explaining why it's been rejected.

If you want to know when your material is received, the Copyright Office suggests sending it by registered or certified mail and requesting a return receipt. Allow at least three weeks for return of your receipt.

Regardless of how long it takes to process your application, copyright registration is effective on the date that your application, fee and deposit are received. Receipt of your certificate of registration is not needed before you publish nor is permission from the Copyright Office needed to place a copyright notice on your material.

The Copyright Office asks that you include your zip code in your return address and that you provide a daytime phone number.

When submitting material for copyright registration, include the non-refundable filing fee, the completed application, and your non-returnable deposit (plus copies, phonorecords, or identifying material) *in the same package.*

# CHAPTER 12

# CHOOSING THE RIGHT TOOLS

Today's computer technology changes hourly. It makes no difference whether we talk about Apples, IBMs, PCs, or clones. The system you install on your desk today will be obsolete in a week's time, maybe less. Someone, somewhere's always going to have a more powerful system than most of us could ever dream of affording. To boot, as computer technology changes, making the choice between one brand of computer over another or one software package over another is becoming more and more a matter of personal preference. While there's still a lot of hype within the computer industry over whether one brand truly is superior to others, the reality from an end user's perspective is that the major differences are becoming fewer and fewer.

From the standpoint only of cost, desktop publishing's not an expensive business to get into. Inexpensive low-end software is available that allows anyone with a computer, a laser printer, a modem and a good eye for visual detail to create 300 dpi publications suitable for clients with certain types of jobs. For those who send work to a service bureau, it's even possible to forego the laser printer, though 300 dpi printers are so inexpensive that it makes little sense to do so, and the advantage of being able to proof decent hardcopy really justifies the investment. Unfortunately, the costs of low-end equipment also allow anyone willing to spend the money on equipment and peripherals to get into the business, even if he or she doesn't have a good eye for what is visually attractive — or at least a basic understanding of design, printing and typography.

# Basic choices

## Low-end systems

Not all older computer systems can be adapted to desktop publishing, but many can be. Several desktop publishers interviewed for this book were using older computers, both in the Macintosh and PC platforms. All reported good results with these older systems even though the machines operate considerably slower than their newer cousins. Many who use the older technology use a modem to link directly to a service bureau to get typeset quality, using a 300 dpi printer solely for proofing, if at all. Some offer 300 dpi work at reduced rates for specific types of work, but only a few reported using 300 dpi exclusively for all jobs.

For desktop publishers starting out with low-end technology, software's a bigger concern, but rapid gains are being made even in this area. Low-end desktop publishing software is available for well under $200. Some of this software is now PostScript and Windows-compatible and offers a tremendous number of options for the price. Still, in most cases it doesn't offer the degree of precision and accuracy or the quality available with medium-range programs such as PageMaker, Ventura Publisher, CorelDRAW, Adobe Illustrator, Aldus Freehand, Arts & Letters or Quark Express, just to name a few. As for printers, some 300 dpi printers put out amazingly good quality but compared to high-resolution imagesetter output under a linen tester or magnifying glass, there's a clear difference even to the untrained eye.

Low-end technology can be a good place to start for someone who wants to try desktop publishing on for size before making a long-term commitment to it as a business and lifestyle. It's also not a bad way to begin if startup funds and capital are limited. In either case, odds are that as the client base grows, so will demands for increasingly sophisticated services that simply cannot be provided by sticking with low-end technology. Street prices for computers in the low-end range is generally $1,200 or less, but anyone buying a computer in this price range for desktop publishing should use caution and make sure it's capable of handling memory-intensive DTP software.

# Medium-range systems

Hardware and software in this category falls from a few to several notches above that of low-end systems. Computers in this range are faster and can do more things than their older counterparts but aren't the most sophisticated state-of-the-art equipment available. Prices for complete computer systems in this range run between $1,200 and $5,000 — more generally toward the higher end. As a rule, software prices range from $400 to a few thousand dollars. Serious desktop publishers can find just about all of their equipment, software and peripheral needs in this range, if desired. Quality computers, printers, scanners and software are all available in this price range. A few thousand dollars invested wisely can create a completely functional desktop publishing setup capable of producing impressive high-quality documents.

For the desktop publisher who has the capital to invest in equipment and who wants to offer quality work, a medium-range system is a sensible choice.

# High-range systems

There may be little difference between the software used for a medium-range and a high-range system except that the software's likely to function more quickly and efficiently under a high-range system. The big difference is that a high-range system includes a state-of-the-art computer designed for individual or network use, and higher-quality scanners and printers are available. Some software designed specifically for desktop publishing also falls into this category and can run into several thousands of dollars in cost. Personally, I think much of this software is starting to go the way of the dinosaurs because so many less expensive software packages now emulate the abilities of this costly software, but some companies that market these expensive solutions manage to keep on hanging in there.

A high-range system is the route to go if spending large sums of money to achieve quality results is no obstacle.

## Ultra high-tech

These are the systems that most of us dream about but few can afford. The systems used by large corporations that have seemingly unlimited working capital to upgrade equipment at any time, even if the existing system's only been in a year or two. Systems like this offer every bell and whistle that's been dreamed up and often are on the cutting edge of technology; sometimes so cutting that the system's not been fully tested and is full of bugs. Large corporations sometimes cut good deals for such systems in exchange for being the "beta test" guinea pigs for an unproven system. But just one component for systems like this can run tens of thousands of dollars, and a complete system can cost hundreds of thousands of dollars. These systems are mentioned only to point out that they exist, since they're beyond the reach of most of us financially as well as beyond the needs of many of us.

# Recommendations

## Choosing a system

As technology changes, so do our definitions of "low-end," "medium-range" and "high-tech" equipment. Prices tend to remain relatively constant for each range, but today's high-tech equipment becomes tomorrow's medium range equipment; today's medium-range hardware and software tomorrow's low-end systems. So how do you decide which option is best?

- For starters, do as much research as possible in the time available. It's better to put off making a purchase for a month or two than to rush out and grab a computer off the shelf just because it's time to upgrade. First, it can take that much time to make intelligent, informed decisions about what's available and what the real needs are. Secondly, postponing a decision often saves money or results in being able to buy a more powerful system for the same amount of money. A system that you'd pay $1,500 for today might sell for $1,200 two months from now. At the same time, don't postpone decisions indefinitely. That only results in current equipment becoming further and further outdated, and if hardware and software hasn't been upgraded regularly, it can reach a point where the equipment's so obsolete that it can't be upgraded at a reasonable price. When that happens, a new system's necessary anyway.
- Know your needs. How critical is it that the computer operate at lightning speed? How much memory is needed to run programs? How much memory does your printer need so that it can handle graphics files efficiently? Is a full-page monitor essential? Desirable? Is a quiet keyboard important? Or a particular keyboard layout? Do you need to access more than one program at a time without having to switch back to your operating system? Do you need to operate programs in the background while you work in a word processor, for example? Do you need to be able to accept different disk sizes? Are you operating a network that includes several computers and peripherals? Do you need a translator so that you can accept disks in a variety of formats, regardless of which platform was used initially?

- Remember that price is not the sole indicator of a product's quality, whether it's a computer, a scanner, a printer or software. If possible, get references of other users of the product and check to see how they like it. Ask specific questions and be sure to ask if there's anything the user doesn't like. Along this line, it also pays to remember that you're always dealing with a salesperson when buying a new computer system and that no matter how friendly or helpful, many computer salespeople work at least partly on commission. When they do, it's in their own financial interest to sell you the most expensive system they can, even if you don't need it.

- Ask about the level of support, length of time for warranties, whether warranties cover parts and labor. Get references of several people who've purchased the same systems or have dealt with the same vendors and check with them about service. Computer salespeople often promise the moon when selling a system, but when it comes time to deliver on the promised verbal warranty, many companies don't shell out even a sliver of moon. Get any promises about warranty and support levels in writing. If there are specific concerns, get them in writing.

- Be absolutely certain before walking out the door with a new system that it will handle any software you want to throw its way and that it meets or exceeds expectations for coping with memory-intensive applications.

- Seriously consider buying quality used equipment, doing so with the same caution you would use in buying a used car. Buying this way can frequently allow you to get exceptional bargains, and may allow you to acquire equipment that is superior to what you can afford new.

Once all these variables have been weighed, buy the best system you can afford, within reason, without depleting all working capital or resources. If you do invest all working capital in equipment and software, realize it can place the business at substantial risk. It's better to slightly overbuy and get a system that you can grow into than to underbuy and be stuck immediately with a system that won't handle even current needs, but a system that's too powerful or expensive can be overkill, and if purchased on terms it can strangle a business.

One of the great things about desktop publishing is that unlike some businesses that require a large capital investment up front, a desktop publishing business can be started with minimal investment in startup costs. Equipment and software can be added as the money's available and as demand dictates. Every desktop publisher has in mind an "ideal" system, and most of us always have "just one or two more items" we'd like to add to have the "perfect" system. Eventually, we add those items, then we learn of something else that would make our work easier. At the very least, though, a serious desktop publisher will want to consider the following: computer system and peripherals; the need for an extra phone line or lines (separate lines used exclusively for business are legitimate deductible business expenses, even if they're in a residence); monitor needs; printer needs; scanner needs; modem and fax needs; and office furnishings and equipment (desks, bookcases, calculators, diskette storage, filing cabinets, etc.).

## Software considerations

The often repeated advice still holds true that before buying a computer system, it pays to know what kind of software you plan to use and how you plan to use it. There's no point in buying an $800 computer with 2 megabytes of RAM, for example, if you plan to use desktop publishing software that requires 4 megabytes of RAM. Nearly all software these days lists system requirements in a readily visible location on the package. Often, compatibility with other software also is listed and some companies even go so far as to list software that's specifically incompatible.

It also pays to know how much total memory all software packages combined will take up on a hard drive. A 40 megabyte hard drive's not adequate if you're software uses most of it. Many of today's programs, especially in the desktop publishing arena, are memory hogs. Disk compression programs can help by doubling a drive's capacity, but some applications or an abundance of programs can push even 800 and 900 megabyte drives.

A desktop publisher's client base will determine the business' focus and the most essential software, but programs that are particularly useful to desktop publishers include word processors, one or more desktop publishing packages, one or more draw programs, a good database (whether to choose a flat or relational database is a decision that can only be made by individual circumstances and needs); a spreadsheet; an accounting program; a label-making program; and time and expense software. Where caller ID service is available, sophisticated database-type software that functions like an instant tickler file also is worth a look.

# When to upgrade

Sooner or later a decision that faces any computer owner is when to upgrade. Or more specifically, when it pays to upgrade vs. pumping more money and time into an existing system. Views on this vary, with some desktop publishers never upgrading unless it's absolutely necessary (because a key piece of equipment broke and can no longer be repaired) and others regularly upgrading hardware and software. I lean toward the latter approach.

Take a $4,500 investment to upgrade hardware and software, for example. Sure, that's a hefty chunk of money to shell out whether you pay it in a lump sum or finance it on terms over a period of time. Spread over the computer's useful life of three to five years, however, that's an investment of between $75 and $125 a month (a little more if financed) for a system that does everything you need it to do, except maybe make the coffee in the morning. That's a pretty low price to pay for the tools of a trade. The sensible business approach is to view upgrades as an investment in your business' future, rather than strictly as a major business expense. Yes, it costs money to upgrade. Maybe we'd rather not spend that money. But experienced businesspeople know it pays to stay competitive, even when it means spending to improve and modernize. With computer-based businesses, this happens more quickly than in many other types of businesses.

"It's going to be the same for any small business," says Elyse Chapman in Claremont, California, "You're always going to have a giant Sears catalog wish list of stuff you want to get. The bottom line is, 'Do you have the money to do that, is it really that prudent, is it really going to improve productivity? When you have the money or see the right opportunity, then change."

It's foolhardy, Chapman says, to make change just for the sake of change "but when you can honestly justify getting the new equipment, then go for it. I upgrade when I see the need to and finances are in line for it and I don't have other places to use the money more prudently." If an upgrade need doesn't line up with other priorities, she says, "then the other priorities take over."

In Westport, Connecticut, Kathleen Tinkel sees "no excuse for a person who's earning a living from desktop publishing not to keep up with upgrades." She points out that technical support often is not available for old software and that usually requirements of newer software drive the need for hardware upgrades.

Several desktop publishers report that they upgrade when it will make their business money. Ron Wodaski of Pittsburgh, Pennsylvania, says, "The business has to pay for the equipment. As long as I can afford it, I'll buy the best I can afford. I try to make the money up front or expand the business to a new area by marketing before investing" in the equipment.

From Des Plaines, Illinois, Rick Ornberg writes, "I try to stay current with technology, or at least as current as my checkbook will allow. As files destined for 'Lino' got larger and larger, for example, I invested in a removable hard drive. I added a color monitor for slide work, and increased memory as needed. Current hardware, however, seems to become nearly obsolete within three or four years, so I try to buy equipment that can handle a lot of expansion and upgrades."

In Hawaii, Charlene Anderson-Shea upgrades equipment and software "all the time. If it wasn't a business, it would be a hobby. If I could afford it, I probably would have all the stuff I have just for fun. I read every computer book and magazine out there and go to MacWorld conferences. I was just at Seybold in October. To me it's not a chore; it's fun to keep up with this stuff."

Not everything about upgrading is hunky-dory, though. Like many of us, Peggy Schillinger of Ann Arbor, Michigan, found it impossible to sell a used computer. "I upgrade much too often," says Peggy. "I bought computers in 1986, 1988, 1989 and 1991. I try to sell my used computers, but the technology is flying by so fast that they really aren't worth much." She adds that in 1991 she tried to sell a used IBM-compatible AT "and ended up donating it to a charity."

Ever changing technology also causes even those of us once comfortable with tearing the insides out of computers to approach upgrades more cautiously. C.J. Metschke of Grayslake, Illinois, worked for United Airlines when PCs were born. "At that time," she says, I knew everything about PCs, how to put chips in, boards, et cetera. Now I am getting more specialized and I'm less concerned with the technology itself. I am coming to rely more on others to set up software and make it work."

Metschke stays current on software but in late 1991 still was using a 286 purchased in 1987. She expected to spend about the same amount of money for an anticipated upgrade but to get "quantum leaps in performance. The basis of my philosophy is to get the biggest, fastest and best (equipment) that I can."

In St. Paul, Minnesota, Heidi Waldmann sums up the paradox in keeping up with computer upgrades, "This type of business is in constant flux. I'm always learning new programs, software, et cetera. Whatever you do, you're always sort of out of date. You need to have a tolerance for it."

Carrying that view into practice, Dennis and Linny Stovall of Blue Heron Publishing, Hillsboro, Oregon, eschew "the bleeding edge of technology." Linny notes that, "we let somebody else buy the latest and greatest at the highest price. We know that the sort of person who does that will be upgrading again at the first opportunity; that's when we buy what they're abandoning at remarkably low prices. Despite not having the 'state of the art,' we're generally ahead of other publishers we know."

# Typesetting vs. DTP

Even with all the technological advances in desktop publishing and printers in recent years, some jobs still require "true" typesetting rather than work created with desktop publishing software and a laser printer. As laser printers and desktop publishing capabilities improve in quantum leaps every six months or so, however, the need for more traditional typesetting becomes less and less. Many clients and companies are finding, too, that they can live with less quality, especially when it means spending less money. Someday, maybe not too far down the road, desktop publishing in the range affordable to most of us is likely to completely replace typesetting technologies that rely on RC papers, films and other expensive phototypesetting technologies. In the meantime, when these services are needed they're as close as a modem call to a service bureau.

# Choosing a service bureau

Finding a good, reliable service bureau — and one that can handle files from your particular hardware and software — can be tricky. Of the dozens of desktop publishers interviewed for this book, at least half a dozen reported their first experiences with service bureaus were either through trial and error or a matter of convenience. For some, the initial steps into the world of desktop publishing and digital typesetting were taken hand-in-hand with a local typesetter. However it's done, though, finding a service bureau doesn't need to be a big, bad, ugly experience.

Even those of us who live in smaller communities are, with today's technology, only a modem call away from service bureaus in the closest large city. If there's no rush, disks can be sent by mail, with copy returned the same way — or even sent directly on to clients.

One of the biggest considerations in seeking a service bureau is compatibility. Some service bureaus work exclusively with Macs; others with PCs. Some work with both. Even if you're working from a different platform, if a PostScript file can be provided many service bureaus can work with it, but not all promise 100 percent compatibility in such cases. More service bureaus seem geared to Macs than to PCs, but since most offer 24-hour turn-around from the time they receive a job, PC users who can't find a service bureau in the closest big city may want to try the next closest large city.

Some desktop publishers do not use, and apparently see no need for, service bureaus. If all of a desktop publisher's clients are satisfied with laser printer output, that's fine, but it does limit income opportunities that can come along unexpectedly. Say, for example, that Jo has earned all her income in two years in business from work she's produced using a high-resolution laser printer. She gets a call one day from Jim at Mr. Right's Seabreeze Tanning Salon, wanting to know about producing a quality full-color brochure. If she's got a lot of experience and the right equipment, maybe Jo can do this in house; maybe not. In either case, it's likely she'd save herself a lot of time, and perhaps money, by using a service bureau for a job like this. The additional cost is often nominal and, in any case, will be passed on to Jo's client.

Besides compatibility, another key to finding a service bureau you can work with is to ask lots of questions. An obvious question to ask is a bureau's software preferences and, by name, whether it refuses to accept files generated from certain software. Kathleen Tinkel also recommends asking specific questions to learn how well the service bureau understands the technology. How does the bureau control density, for example. Another question to ask might be how the bureau copes with problem blends? What does it do about banding? Will it help solve the problem, or simply blame it on your software? Of course, asking these questions presumes some technical knowledge on the part of the desktop publisher, and not everyone claiming to be a desktop publisher has this technical knowledge.

This lack of technical knowledge carries over into some service bureaus and is another reason for asking a lot of questions. "I find it very frightening," says C.J. Metschke, "when I'm talking with someone and I find I know more than they do. There are a lot of service bureaus that don't know how to handle files born on an IBM." Metschke adds that she's found a couple of service bureaus in Chicago that "really know their stuff."

Andy White of L.grafix, a service bureau in Portland, Oregon, says that software "gets put to the final test" when it goes to a bureau. "The most common thing we hear," he says, "is 'well, it worked on my laser printer.' When it goes to the imagesetter, that's not always the case." A good service bureau, though, will work with first-time customers to resolve such problems as well as offer suggestions on how to set up files to achieve desired results. Some experimentation may be necessary, since specifications used to set a 2-point rule on a laser printer may bring completely different results on an imagesetter, where the line may come out thicker or thinner and with more or less margin than allowed for in laser printer output. It makes sense, therefore, to choose a service bureau before it's needed rather than in the midst of an important job when the client insists on higher-quality type.

Yet another reason to ask lots of questions is to determine the right type of service bureau for your needs. White notes there are bureaus that simply process disks to finished output; others that take the approach that they're more than just processors and provide typesetting, design and color separation services; and still others that offer high-end scanning and other high-tech services. "Depending on the need, it's important to know the skill level of the people you're working with and how much assistance you might expect to have as you run into obstacles," he says. "It may be, for one particular printer, the guy who just processes film is absolutely adequate." On the other hand, a graphic artist doing four-color brochures on the desktop may need a bureau where the entire piece can be output at one time.

White also recommends talking with the service bureau before starting a job. "People can put a lot of time in before getting to the service bureau and then be disappointed."

All service bureaus "do essentially the same thing," White says, "so what we have to offer is a level of service that's comprised both of turnaround time and service provided on quality, checking, prices, et cetera. To a lot of people, the ability to get something out in a short period of time is more important than cost."

He also emphasizes the importance of understanding the tools of desktop publishing and service bureaus. "It seems you can't just pour things in there without knowing the repercussions. You have to understand fonts, how they're used, what should go where, how to organize, how to back up. These kinds of things are as fundamental as knowing what different traffic signs are when driving a car.

"If you're going to be dealing in screened images, you need a basic understanding of lines per inch, dots per inch and pixels per inch. Maybe in some cases, having some idea of what an imagesetting device is, knowing how to prepare files properly."

A good service bureau, White notes, will offer desktop publishers help in these areas when it's needed.

Finally, another area not to overlook when asking questions in the quest for a service bureau is pricing. Many service bureaus offer price breaks when work is ordered in quantity; it may pay to group different jobs together to get the price break. At the same time, oversized documents, complex graphics or unanticipated work that's needed to clean up files and make them workable will affect the final price.

## Tools of the future

In the world of desktop publishing there's one certainty and that is that technology will continue evolving at a pace that's at times incomprehensible. Basic principles of good design don't seem likely to change as much or as quickly as the technological tools we use, tools likely to be obsolete within a couple of years — almost certainly within five. Previews of state-of-the-art equipment at Seybold and similar events offer glimpses into what the future holds for desktop publishers, but no one can say with absolute certainty that some as yet undiscovered technological breakthroughs will not surface and again alter forever the way we approach our task of making things look good on the printed page.

# CHAPTER 13

# ADDING DOLLARS THROUGH DIVERSITY

Professional writers who work on a freelance basis, even successful ones, know the hit and miss nature of relying on income from this type of work. Book sales and royalties offer a more stable income base, but unlike paychecks, royalty checks don't come in every couple of weeks and even successful writers can have months or years of sales followed by months or years of constant rejection slips. Established writers also get rejection slips regularly, and it's a prime reason that many seek out agents to market their work. That way the writer can concentrate on work without facing daily the inevitable rejection that's a part of the business.

Because of the up and down nature of the writing business, it's not surprising that many writers have turned to desktop publishing for a regular income base to supplement the good times and carry them through the bad. Desktop publishing is fun. It provides the contact with people that writers crave but seldom have time for during writing projects. And, once established, a desktop publishing business allows many writers to work full-time in writing-related fields. The only complaint comes from writers whose DTP businesses flourish: they're so busy with projects for others that they don't have time to write.

Not all writers are cut out to be desktop publishers, nor are all desktop publishers meant to be writers. It has always amazed me that some writers can't design and some designers can't write, since when you get right down to the nitty gritty, words on paper are nothing more than a set of symbols arranged on a page that send a signal to the brain, which then translates it into images and ideas — in other words, a picture. To illustrate, if we substitute "hogs on a rooftop" for "words on paper" in the previous sentence, our brain instantly sends us a much different, and patently absurd, visual image of what's going on. In any case, writers who can't design and desktop publishers who can't write can find it mutually beneficial to refer work to one another and even to work together, formally or informally, on projects. It can add dollars to the coffers that otherwise might not ever be there.

What does all this about writing have to do with desktop publishing? Not much, except to illustrate that branching out into other areas can add significant revenue sources and help put on a solid footing a business that, with only one income source, might be on shaky ground. Expanding into new areas of service isn't a technique used only by writers. Successful businesses have known for years that one of the best safeguards against losses that can force a company out of business is to offer a diversity of services and/or to invest in a variety of companies. That's one of the major reasons that many large retailers own several types of retail outlets, instead of just one, and an underpin of why community newspaper ownership in today's society generally is more economical under group ownership.

This doesn't mean that a desktop publisher who's never lived anywhere but in a large city should necessarily go out and buy a pig farm just to keep from putting all eggs in one basket. Even when diversifying, it's best to stick with things you know unless you're a glutton for learning things the hard way.

# Making the best choices

Desktop publishers who offer only one or two services, say graphic design and newsletters, are limiting their opportunities. When times are good, this isn't likely to be much of a problem and the money will roll in on a more or less regular basis. When economies change, though, and they always do sooner or later no matter where you live, the company offering only one or two services can face tough times unless it adapts quickly. A better approach is to consider your expertise, experience and interests and decide beforehand which services are compatible with the type of desktop publishing service you want to offer. At the very least, this means preparing a mental list of interests, activities, experience, expertise, goals and objectives. More likely, it will work better if the list is prepared with pencil and paper or on computer. Software packages are available to help with this type of planning but word processors and spreadsheets that allow looks at "what if" situations work just fine.

One helpful technique for deciding what services are compatible with those already offered is to divide a sheet of paper into two columns, or use two sheets of paper. On one, list all the things you like to do. Everything. The kinds of work you like, hobbies, interests, whether you like to be around people, the kinds of animals you like, et cetera. On the other, list everything you don't like to do. Don't be selective with either list at first; that's the next step.

When finished, most of us will have filled at least each column; for some, the lists may take several pages. Now it's time to start the selection process, by elimination. Usually, it's easy to eliminate most of the things we don't like to do from the list of services we want to offer, but there may be one or two that make sense and aren't really odious. From the remaining list, put in order the top five or ten that are most enjoyable. This provides a base from which to work in deciding on compatible services.

Many businesses simply add the services at this point, acting on hunch or gut instinct. Sometimes there's simply a clear need in a community that's going unmet and the first business that picks up on the need has the edge, for a while anyway. Acting on a hunch sometimes makes businesses lots of money, but the prudent thing to do at this point is market research. This takes time, but needn't be expensive. A well-designed questionnaire or a telephone survey of potential clients can provide much information about their needs, as can a survey of services offered by competitors. Response may be small — out of a mailing to 500 potential clients only 10 to 15 may reply, but the information gleaned from those respondents can be enough to help refine a decision about adding services. Maybe someone else already offers the same service and there's little room for you, or maybe there's an untapped potential in an area you hadn't thought of. Another way to test the market for new services is by placing ads in publications known to bring response for existing services or to spread the word among existing clients that new services are available.

Another good indicator of when to add services is when clients request them. In my business, if market research showed demand for a new service, I wouldn't wait until customers requested it. I'd simply add it and start marketing the service to existing clients, because if clients already use one service they usually need others. On the other hand, clients suggest services that I've never thought about and might not have thought about had they not suggested them. It's always possible in such situations to offer custom quotes for the work on a one-time basis, but if over one or two months I get half a dozen requests for the same service it's time to take a serious look at whether to add it.

As much as we might like it to be, adding services isn't as easy as simply deciding what we like to do and then doing a little market research. A new service needs to also make sense financially. If new equipment is needed, the investment needs to pay for itself. The new service also needs to contribute to the business' profit. Otherwise there's no point in adding the service. Again, software is available that offers help in this area of planning, and spreadsheets are another valuable analysis tool. Many business books are available, offering a variety of formulas to evaluate a new service in light of current competition and the state of the business. And self-help courses oriented to businesses are available through community colleges, university continuing education programs or through other local organizations. Experienced businesspeople often use several formulas, not just one, in weighing whether to add a new service. The tremendous variety of formulas available is beyond the scope of this book, but I've tried to include some reliable, current sources in the resource list advertised in the back of the book.

When it comes to adding services, few of us make perfect decisions every time. Even using different accepted "what if" approaches with spreadsheets, all the facts and figures can show that a service should be profitable yet when it is offered it proves a financial drain. Other times, a service that on paper is marginal or a money loser becomes one of our most profitable areas. Even with today's sophisticated analytical financial tools, there's always some degree of second-guessing about what will fly with clients and what won't. Subjective factors cannot be ignored.

There's always some degree of risk and sometimes we must take chances or go with "gut feelings" regardless of facts and figures. The degree of risk employees are willing take when working for a company not only affects the firm's bottom line but it can affect the employee's tenure. Sometimes companies grow stale because employees aren't willing to take enough risks. For the self-employed person working independently, the degree of risk inevitably affects the bottom line for good or bad, since the "middleman" employee no longer enters the picture.

# Possible compatible services

A list of additional services that can be compatible with desktop publishing is provided on the opposite page to help get the creative juices flowing. It's by no means comprehensive and simply illustrates the tremendous variety of options available. Whether these or other services are compatible with any desktop publishing service depends on individual experience, interests, finances and competition.

# Narrowing the selection

For some companies, the choice is not how to diversify through additional services but how to selectively narrow the range of services so that there's still a good income base without spreading the workload so thin that there's not time to do everything. While not limited to the home-based one- and two-person operations, it's a problem common to businesses of this type. Some desktop publishers cope with it simply by adding hours to their work day, doing mostly marketing during the day and the actual work after hours. Jeanne MacGregor of LaserType in Bellingham, Washington, admits that she "gets pretty overloaded sometimes. I just work longer hours." She adds that having a fax machine has made a big difference.

Others, like Carol Pentleton, simply limit their services, set their fees higher and concentrate only on the most profitable areas. "I have limited my services by getting rid of all the stuff that I am personally not comfortable with or is not profitable or enjoyable," Pentleton says, "Thus, I no longer paint handmade signs, or do advertising for political clients or jewelry manufacturers or car dealers."

Another approach is to market until there's enough work to keep busy for several months, then worry about new clients and projects when the current ones are completed. This approach works, but it leads to an inevitable cycle of fat months followed by lean months, and it's an approach that most of us would prefer to avoid — and can avoid — with more consistent attention to marketing. Peggy Schillinger of Advanced Technical Communications markets herself as "a technical writer who can deliver camera-ready desktop-published pages" but she admits that she does very little marketing and "unfortunately, I've had some lean months as a result. I advertise in a local freelancer's directory and I am listed in the Yellow Pages. Both of these sources produce very few leads. I get most of my leads because I am well-networked into the technical writing market locally."

From the outside, the perception is often that desktop publishing is easy, but regardless of which approach desktop publishers choose to keep from spreading the workload too thin, few report working only a forty-hour week. For most of us, the workload runs into sixty- to seventy-hour weeks, even if we hold down another part-time job. The trade-off, at least for those of us who work from home, is that we have at least some control over which hours we work.

Like many of us, MacGregor started business with "just enough money to buy a computer. I just jumped into the pool with both feet and started swimming as fast as I could. I've had a number of young women talk to me about how easy it would be to do this. It's not easy. You have to know what you're doing.

"I had to work hard. Before I started I had a business degree and several years of working as a secretary in the fields of banking, finance, real estate, architecture, law and education.

"They say you should always market, especially at the peak of your workloads. Most of my marketing is through networking. In effect, I'm marketing all day long. I often make the comment that I don't get much done Monday through Friday from 9 to 5. The actual work is after hours."

One other way to avoid spreading yourself too thin is to take only a predetermined number of clients. The danger here is that any business loses clients over time. Such losses sometimes are beyond our control, due to death of a client or a move, for example. A business that loses several clients in a short period of time, and that hasn't constantly been marketing its services, can find the going rough — especially if the economy has gone from good to sour. It takes time to find new clients, and that, in turn, takes time away from income-producing work.

For a desktop publisher, or any other small-business owner, staying busy is never a problem. Staying busy and bringing in enough money to keep the wolves away from the door can be. Diversifying services (without spreading the workload so thin that we don't do a good job at anything) is one positive step toward alleviating this problem.

# POSSIBLE DIRECTIONS FOR DIVERSIFICATION

Accounting/bookkeeping

Advertising copywriting

Advertising sales

Billing service

Book editing

Book publishing

Columnist

Communications consulting

Computer consulting

Consulting to self-publishers

DTP training

Database management

Editorial services

Fact checking

Ghostwriting

Grant writing

Indexing service

Information brokering

Lecturing

Literary agenting

Magazine editing and publishing

Mailing list brokering

Manuscript preparation & consulting

Marketing

Media placement

Newsletter consulting

Newsletter publishing

Newspaper consulting

Newspaper publishing

Office organizing

Photography

Pre-press services

Print brokering

Proofreading

Public relations

Publication consulting

Publishing workshops

Researching

Service bureau

Software programming & development

Speechwriting

Teaching/tutoring

Technical writing/editing

Temporary help agency

Translating computer disks

Translating languages

Typography consultant

Word processing

Writing

# CHAPTER 14

# FINDING THE LOOPHOLES

When one's in business there are always loopholes, legitimate and otherwise, for circumventing rules, regulations and laws. In some cases, just finding the loopholes could be a full-time job in itself. I don't recommend this approach, since there are more profitable ways to spend one's time than looking for every shortcut available. At the same time, it can pay to be on the lookout for time- and money-saving loopholes.

## Legitimate loopholes

The best of these, of course, are legitimate breaks that may take some close digging through the gobbledygook of tax bureaucratese.

## Tax breaks

A lot of tax breaks exist for traditional and home-based businesses, and as long as you're operating a legitimate business it makes sense to claim these deductions. It doesn't make sense, on the other hand, to fail to take the deductions because of fear of a tax audit or because you don't think it's right to claim the deductions. One of the earliest lessons a businessperson can learn is that different tax rules apply to businesses than to individuals, and failure to claim even one legitimate deduction can make a big difference not only on your tax bill but also on your bottom line profit or loss. Chances are that competitors will claim the deduction even if you don't, and that can give them an edge.

Those new to the business world also often worry about the need to constantly show a profit. Unless the business shows steady negative cash flow over a long period, this really shouldn't be much of a concern. For starters, few new businesses show immediate, or consistent gross profits during their first years. Secondly, even well-run businesses often show good gross profits but have only a marginal after-tax net profit or an after-tax net operating loss once legitimate deductions are claimed. The IRS makes it fairly easy on new, unincorporated businesses, stipulating that a business can show a loss for "x" number of years in a specified period of time. (Check with the local IRS office or an accountant for current rules). Additionally, even if losses exceed terms designated by the IRS, leniency is often granted if intent to make a profit can be shown through business records.

It might seem strange that a taxing body would show such leniency, but it's really in its own best interest to do so. Given enough time, many businesses become profitable, adding to the country's tax base. Successful businesses also tend to grow. That often means hiring employees and that, in turn, again strengthens the tax base, especially when it provides jobs that otherwise would not exist.

Rather than worry about the need to constantly show a profit, a more sensible approach is to focus on the overall, long-term stability and profitability of a company. Ideally, a startup company either has money in the bank or its owner has another income source to carry it through until the business starts showing a profit. Even barring that, as long as the business is paying its bills and the owner's able to pay the mortgage or rent, put food on the table and cover medical expenses, it doesn't make a whole lot of sense to worry about short-term profit. Even long-established businesses often show seasonal or occasional monthly operating losses. Careful attention to management of a business for long-term profitability requires a different set of skills and knowledge than that needed for its day-to-day management. Many owners of one-person businesses do not have both sets of skills, and this is where a carefully selected group of trusted advisers can be of help. For businesspeople interested in acquiring these skills, help is available through SBA publications, numerous business books and publications, workshops and seminars, classes at community colleges and universities, as well as from consultants.

## Legitimate tax loopholes

Occasionally in the drafting and rewriting of tax laws, law-makers overlook some area of potential tax revenues. When this happens it's legal, and widely accepted business practice, to use the loophole to full advantage. Again, it doesn't make sense to reject taking such a deduction because it "wasn't the intent" of the lawmakers. Even if we sat through the entire process of writing tax laws, how many of us could truly say later that we know the true "intent" of any lawmaking body? Not only that, but if lawmakers didn't want businesses to claim deductions resulting from such a loophole, they should have been more careful about drafting and rewriting the tax law in the first place.

## Paying the penalty

Whether they're state, federal or local, nearly all taxing bodies impose penalties for late payments. Sometimes these penalties are substantial, other times they're in line with or close to the charges that would be imposed for late payment on a standard charge account. Consistent late payment of taxes isn't something I'd recommend, but occasionally a late payment can make sense and sometimes there's simply no choice. If the money isn't there, it isn't there. New businesses, especially, tend to face this latter problem but it also can strike a company experiencing rapid growth or a company whose revenues suddenly take a nose-dive following a period of growth.

Even when the money is there, though, it sometimes makes more sense to spend it elsewhere and briefly postpone payment of taxes. If, for example, you're offered an extremely good price for some much-needed equipment or software, the amount you pay as a penalty for late payment of taxes may be more than off-set by the savings on the equipment purchase. Each situation must be weighed on its own merits, of course, and if the money's available to both pay the taxes and purchase the equipment, that's the most sensible thing to do. But if it comes down to a choice between the two and you know money's coming in shortly that will allow payment of the taxes, making the purchase can be a sensible decision. In most cases, you're not going to be hauled off to the local hoosegow just because you didn't pay your taxes on time.

# Working with creditors and vendors

Sooner or later every business faces a cash crunch, even those that operate on a cash accounting basis. Businesses that have established solid relationships with creditors and vendors may have an edge in such cases. While delaying payments to creditors and vendors may not be a true "loophole," it can give a business a competitive edge. The best approach is to take the initiative and contact the creditors and vendors to explain the situation, how long it's expected to last, and what payment arrangements can be made in the interim. Creditors and vendors often are surprisingly flexible in such instances, provided they're not experiencing a cash crunch problem themselves.

# Questionable practices
## Tax deductions

Despite what the IRS and other tax-making authorities would like us to believe, tax laws aren't always clearcut and there's often room for interpretation. On the federal level, since tax laws were rewritten in the mid-1980s, many tax situations are open to debate. Whether to claim deductions in these instances depends largely on how much risk you're willing to run of an audit. Some CPAs and financial advisers urge a conservative approach and suggest claiming only deductions known to fall within the parameters of long-established legitimacy. Others take the approach that all possible deductions should be claimed and that they always can be disallowed if there is an audit. Many take a moderate approach that falls somewhere between these extremes. In any case, when questionable deductions are claimed, they should be backed up with as much documentation as possible, including receipts, dates, how the deduction relates to business use, etc.

# Business ethics

In business in general, and in desktop publishing specifically, situations often arise that create potential ethical dilemmas. Is it ethical, for example, to be creating political campaign material for candidates while also working as a public information officer on a retainer basis for the city council? Or to accept a major brochure project from a client when you're already doing a similar project for a direct competitor? Can you in all honesty say there's no conflict of interest if you're putting together promotional material for an environmental organization at the same time that you're ghostwriting a book for a client who's lambasting environmental causes? To me, the answer to all the situations listed here is a clear "no," but other situations arise on a regular basis where the answer isn't so clear. Each desktop publisher must decide for him- or herself what is ethical and what isn't, then have the courage and resolve to stand up to clients who are adamant about having things their own way because "money can buy everything."

It's tempting sometimes, especially if the money's really needed, to go with the flow and accept a job that's questionable or that borders on the unethical. In my experience, though, a business is money ahead to keep everything above board and following sound ethical practices. My set of values may be different from those of a desktop publisher down the road, but there is common ground that we all tread that serves to establish some ethical boundaries within which we all should operate. Knowing our own values, and those generally accepted within the industry, also helps establish when it's okay to stretch the rules and when it's time to simply refuse the work.

# Illegal practices

It doesn't take a genius to know that there's been an underground economy for years, and that money earned in this underground economy is never, or at least rarely, reported as taxable income. Only a fool would condone in print a practice that's clearly illegal. Yet the reality is that despite repeated tightening of tax laws by the IRS, an underground economy flourishes in the United States, and it's not all due to drug trafficking.

Clearly, one of the easiest ways to join the underground economy is to simply start doing business from home and never bother to obtain the proper permits or to report income earned in this way to anyone. Equally as clearly, anyone who does this runs certain risks: The risk that eventually some governmental agency will catch up and demand payment of back taxes, a situation that literally can put an end to business; the risk that a client or neighbor will report business activities to the IRS or to governmental agencies from which permits are required; and the risk of being unable to get insurance if you've been reported as operating a business illegally.

We all know people like this, who openly flaunt the tax system and who don't believe in following any government regulations, no matter what they are. Whether it's because of fear of getting nabbed or out of a sense of moral obligation, most of us follow the rules most of the time. Few of us can claim to follow all laws all the time. It's too easy to drive just five miles over the speed limit "because everyone else is doing it." In fact, in some locales, you can even be fined for not driving five miles over the speed limit because failure to keep up with what everyone else is doing "impedes the flow of traffic." Still, there are thousands of Americans who work from home who may report income they earn from home-based operations but who do not bother to get required permits and licenses. In some cases, it's simply lack of knowledge. In others, it's a conscious decision made for any number of reasons, including that home-based work permits are too restrictive, that the permit process is too long and cumbersome, or that working from home simply is not a permitted activity.

Some governments are more responsive than others to the needs of a changing society, but whenever possible it's best to work from within the system to effect change. It may take longer to accomplish this way, but the effects of the change can be more lasting than by simply ignoring the law.

# Keeping secrets

While not really a "loophole," keeping secrets can be important to a company's financial health. A management philosophy gaining currency in recent years is that employees should be told everything about a business' operations and management decisions. The underlying rationale behind this position is that an informed employee is less likely to damage a company's reputation by spreading false information. Not a bad idea, except that a disgruntled employee will use only the information suitable to the purpose and ignore any other information about the company that's been made available. Not every management decision about a company should be a matter of public knowledge; in the wrong hands, such information can prove disastrous. Even publicly-owned companies don't let their stockholders in on every single business decision that's made each day. For one thing, to do so would be impossible. For another, the company's managers are hired for expertise in their particular fields. It's equally as impossible in a small business to advise every employee or sub-contractor of all business decisions; to do so simply wastes valuable time better spent on revenue-producing projects.

Regular meetings with staff, partners or corporate officers are important to discuss larger issues that may affect specific projects or company policies, but a sense of fair play and when to keep silent can go a long way toward keeping a company on solid financial ground.

# CHAPTER 15

# WHERE TO GO FROM HERE

This book has explored many basic business issues and addressed several topics of concern specifically to desktop publishers, writers, and home-based and small businesses. As with any book in today's information-laden society, however, it's not possible to cover every issue of interest in depth.

Some general conclusions can be drawn from the overall context of this book. Foremost, that desktop publishing will continue to change as technology improves at ever-increasing speeds and its price continues to drop, making it essential for the desktop publisher to constantly be looking at equipment and software upgrades in order to remain competitive. Costs often will prevent us from having the most state-of-the-art equipment available, but for 90 percent of the jobs we do, this equipment's not necessary anyway, and when it is, our friendly service bureau's just a phone call away.

It also became clear as I interviewed for this book that large numbers of desktop publishers were blissfully ignorant of potential legal problems that could put a stranglehold on their business in short order. Sometimes it's not so bad to be blissfully ignorant, but when it comes to issues like libel, copyright infringement and invasion of privacy, that's not the case. A good working knowledge of potential problems may help thwart a more serious situation. If this book helps just one desktop publisher realize that it's not all just fun and games in the real world of business, especially in the legal arena, I'll feel as if it's done its job.

As the concept for this book developed over the past few years, it became increasingly evident that I wasn't the only one seeking answers about what works and what doesn't in this relatively new industry. Dozens of "how-to" books are on the market that focus on the technical and design sides of the business. Many of these, though released only a few years ago, continue to grace library shelves though they're already outdated because of technological advances. Few books, however, address the business side of desktop publishing and issues unique to the industry from this perspective.

As tempting as it's been to address the equipment and technical side of desktop publishing, we've intentionally kept discussions of hardware and software as generic as possible, with the realization that technology is changing so fast that anything discussed today is likely to be obsolete within months. Specific mentions of software and hardware in this book are not meant to imply that these products are any better or worse than others on the market. Some examples merely are better illustrated through mention of specifics than through a strictly generic discussion.

Marketing's an area that few of us are naturally good at, but it's one of the most important areas of business. What it really boils down to is the need to be honest with ourselves and potential clients about the capabilities of ourselves and our equipment. Even though many of us may work from home, we can't expect to find clients by holing up there and waiting for the phone to ring. With the rare exception, that just doesn't happen. In the course of our marketing, when all else is said and done, we still have to ask for the business. The best sales pitch in the world isn't going to work if Jack spends half an hour listening, then is told to have a nice day as you walk out the door without asking whether he wants a newsletter or brochure.

The better you get to know a potential client, the better your chances of doing business if there's not a personality clash. People like doing business with people they like, and naturally they like people who are concerned enough to ask about the kids by name, the antics of the family dog, hobbies or interests. In smaller communities, participation in the daily coffee klatch is almost expected if you plan to do business with others in town; in the smallest of towns, it may be a matter of economic survival.

Though it may not be as exciting or satisfying, the experienced businessperson pays as much attention to the business side of desktop publishing as to the fun stuff. Alternatively, the desktop publisher may realize that the attention to detail needed on that side of the business isn't really his or her cup of tea and seek another solution, perhaps subcontracting the work, hiring a book-keeper, taking on a partner, or farming the work out to the company's accountant.

Experienced desktop publishers don't waste time with the nickel-and-dime jobs that seem to lurk around every corner. To do so is an open invitation to frustration — and even dissatisfaction on the part of these clients who, though they're expecting to pay little, often want the equivalent of high-resolution type and who can get irate if they don't get it.

Space limitations, along with questions of currency, make it impossible to include the type of resource list being requested by the dozens of people who took large chunks of time out of their busy schedules to talk with me about this book. So rather than not have one at all, it's been put together separately and may be ordered by filling out the coupon at the back of this book.

Finally, I don't claim to have all the answers to every business situation. The desktop publishing industry is too varied for any one person to know everything there is to know. Businesses, too, operate in different fashions and what works for one may not work for another. Rules and regulations are different from place to place, as are accepted trade practices and prices. Management styles vary and there's no one "right way" to approach running a business. I do hope that my experiences and the experience and knowledge shared by others throughout this book has offered at least some guidance to the often complex decisions that business owners must make daily, often with far less time than we'd like.

# INDEX

©. *See* Copyright

A/P   49, 55
A/R   49, 52
Accountants, choosing   112
Accounts payable   55
Accounts receivable   11, 52, 76
  collecting   58
  financing   81
Advertising   5, 27
  newspapers   27
  word of mouth   19
  Yellow Pages   23
Agreements   102
All Rights   110
Anderson-Shea, Charlene   15, 27, 160
Arntzen-Reynolds   89
Assets   54
Attitude   2
Attorneys   108
  choosing   112
  hiring   108
  libel   118

Bad design
  client requests   90
  refusing jobs   90
Bank accounts   10
Banks   75, 81
Bartering   61
Berne Convention   137
Billing   46, 53
  procedures   10, 11
  software   47
  time   47
Billing system   11
Blue Heron Publishing   35
Bluelines   102
Boe, David   15, 28
Burgoon, Lora   21
Business bank accounts   10
Business basics   49
Business cards   38
Business closures   10
Business diversification   166–172
Business ethics   178
Business groups   9
Business law   108
Business licenses   6

Business names   30
Business plan   10, 11, 58
   credit policy   11
   marketing   11
   billing procedures   11
   credit policies   11
   internal policies   11
Business planning   4
Business stationery   37
Business value   54
Businesses
   home-based   14
   part-time   14
   family-owned   107
   protecting   107

Capital   7
Caricatures, libel   116
Cartoons, libel   116
Cash flow   7, 10, 76, 78, 83
   and marketing   61
   cycles   12
   definition   11
   management   61
   problems   56
   projections   11
Cataloging in Publication
      data   106
Chamber of Commerce   20
Chapman, Elyse   66, 73, 89, 159
Charging interest   54
Choice Words & Graphics   15
Choosing professional help   112
CIP data   106
Client education   69
Client expectations   64, 91
Client responsibilities   103
Clients
   interviewing   92, 94
   limited budgets   95
   problems with   63–73
   self-publishers   105
Clip art, copyright   141
Co-authorship   147
Cold calling   9, 25
Collection agencies   60
Collection letters   60

Collections   11, 58
   attorneys   60
   small claims court   61
Commercial Factors   76
Competitors   20
   knowing   95
   networking with   20
   subcontracting   95
Computer technology   151
   selecting   152–154
   software   157
   upgrading   158
Con artists   66
Consultants   24
   choosing   112
Contracts   68, 101–103
   accountability   101
   client responsibilities   103
   documented terms   101
   indemnification clause   120
   jobs gone wrong   101
   legal review   109
   mutual expectations   101
   oral   101
   proofsheets   101
   trade practices   101
Contribution to a collective
      work   145
Copyright   105, 106
   three basic assumptions   137
   Library of Congress   140
   notice optional   137
   protection   136
   technological changes   136
      4, 109
   automatic granting   110
   Berne Convention   137
   clip art   141
   co-authorship   147
   contribution to a collective
      work   145
   copies of the work   150
   duration   139
   effective date   150
   filing fee   150
   ideas   146
   infringement   135, 143

law prior to 1978    138
litigation    138
on fliers    111
on in-house publications    111
on manuscripts    110
on newsletters    111
Pan Am Copyright
   Convention    138
period of ownership    136
permissions    139, 140, 146
photocopies    142
problem areas    142
public domain    140
registration    111, 149
registration optional    137
subcontracted work    145
titles    146
Universal Copyright
   Convention    138
work for hire    136
work in tangible form    137
Copyright page    139
Copyrighted material
   quoting from    139
   theft of    110
CPAs, choosing    112
Craft    89
Credit    77, 78
   checking    79
   policies    10, 11
   problems    177
   factoring    83
Creditors, problems with    177
Customer relations    8
Customer satisfaction    90
*Cut and Paste*    22

Data Search Publications    22
Design    86
   attitudes toward    4
   subjective nature    91
Design for Print Studio    64
Desktop publishing
   potential    2
   starting    2
Direct contact    9
Direct mail    22

Disclaimer, use of    120
Dornbos, Jim    43, 68

Edwards, Paul and Sarah    4–14,
   24, 46, 53, 108
eec productions    89
Electronic bulletin board
   services    20
Employees    96
   IRS regulations    96
Equipment expenditures    11
Expenses    11

Factoring    4, 75, 82–85
   cash flow    83
   costs of    82
   credit rating    83
Family-owned businesses    107
Fees, setting    4
Finances    10
   separating personal from
      business    7
Financing    74, 80
   accounts receivable    81
   factoring    4, 75, 82
   inventory loan    81
   line of credit    81
   time loan    81
First Amendment    116, 121
First North American Serial
   Rights    109
First Serial Rights    109
Flat fee    44
Fliers, copyrights    111
Foreign Serial Rights    109

Galley proof. *See* Proofsheets
Garno, Brenda    15
Giving out free information    24
Growth
   dangers    55
   planning for    58

Hart, David    76
High-resolution    92
Hinkle, Don    42

Hiring
  by the project   99
  seasonally   99
Home occupation permit   7
Home-based businesses   14
Hopkinson, Stephanie   25
Hourly rate   44
Hughes, Bob   135

Ibis   15
Illegal jobs   67
Illegal practices   179
In-house publications
  copyrights   111
Indemnification clauses   120
Independent contractors   96
  IRS regulations   96
Insurance, libel   125
    group policies   129
Intellectual property law   135
Internal company policies   11
International Standard Book
    Number   105
Interning   89
Interviews
  Anderson-Shea, Charlene   15
  Burgoon, Lora   21
  C.J. Metschke   15
  Chapman, Elyse   66, 89
  David Boe   15
  Edwards, Paul and Sarah   4, 14,
    24, 53, 108
  Garno, Brenda   15
  Hopkinson, Stephanie   25
  MacGregor, Jeane   15
  McGreal, Shirley   119
  Nelson, Marshall   116
  Pentleton, Carol   15
  Scarano, Jane   22
  Dornbos, Jim   43
  Hart, David   76
  Hinkle, Don   42
  Hughes, Bob   135
  Montgomery, Charles C.   64
  Ornberg, Rick   43
  Reynolds, Rob and Audrey
    Arntzen   89

Riviera, Daniel J.   117
Sanford, Bruce W.   116
Stovall, Dennis & Linny   35
Tinkel, Kathleen   29
Waldmann, Heidi   15
White, Andy   163
Wilf, Frederic M.   135
Wodaski, Ron   65
Wunderlich, Judi   29
Invasion of privacy   4, 130. See
    also Libel
  defenses against   134
  model releases   131
  photos   131
Inventory loan   81
ISBN (International Standard Book
    Number)   105
ISBN U.S. Agency   105

Jobs gone wrong, contracts   101

Key man insurance   108

L.grafix   163
LaserType   15
LCC number   105
Legal issues   4, 148
Legal software   108
Letterheads   37
Liabilities   55
Libel   4, 115
  constitutional protection   121
  cost of   118
  defending against   119, 122,
    124
  definition   116
  disclaimer   115, 120
  fair comment   124
  hiring an attorney   118
  indemnification clause   120
  insurance   125, 128
    group policies   129
    premiums   129
    sources   128
  invasion of privacy   130
  opinion   124

photos & graphics 116
privileged communication 123
protecting clients 122
reference works 125
unintentional errors 117
Library of Congress 106
checking copyright 140
copyright registration 111
Library of Congress Catalog
number 105
Licenses 7
Line of credit 81
Litigation, copyright 138
Loans 10, 81
Local businesses as newsletter
clients 26
Local custom 9
Long-term relationships 8
Loopholes 174
legitimate 174
tax breaks 174
Low-resolution 92

MacGregor, Jeanne 15
Mailings
follow-up 9
targeted 9
Major clients, reliance on 17
Management styles 185
Market niche 4
defining 15, 16
periodic review 16
Market research 10
Marketing 4, 8, 17, 105
and cash flow 61
telephone 22
cold calling 25
direct mail 22
giving out free information 24
in Yellow Pages 23
naming the business 36
networking 20
personal contact 22
personal service 17
referrals 28
scheduling 18
self-generating business 19

techniques 18
telephoning 38
through local printers 26
to local businesses 26
using brochures 37
using business cards 38
using newsletters 37
volunteer work 25
word-of-mouth 19
Yellow Pages for prospects 29
Marketing strategy 8
McGreal, Shirley 119
Media Weavers 35
Memberships in business groups 9
Metschke, C.J. 15, 27, 28, 70,
160
Milton, Chad 119
Mistakes, dealing with them 73
Model release 131
example 132
getting 133
requiring 133
Monterey Press Inc., The 15
Montgomery, Charles C. 64
Motion Picture Rights 110

Nelson, Marshall 116
Networking 20
competitors 20
Networks 9
Newsletter Repair 27
Newsletters
as marketing tools 37
copyrights 111
Newspaper advertising 27

Observing local custom 9
One-time Rights 109
Oral contracts 101
Organizations 9, 20
Ornberg & Associates, Rick 43,
46
Ornberg, Rick 51, 90, 159
Output quality 91

Part-time businesses 5, 14

Part-time employees   98
Partnerships   107
Past due accounts
   charging interest   54
   collecting   58
   small claims court   61
Payables   49, 55
Payment terms   50, 53, 76
Pentleton, Carol   15, 21, 25, 72, 90
Personal contact   7, 22
Photographs, libel   116
Photos
   invasion of privacy   131
   model releases   131
Pricing methods   4, 40, 44
Pro bono work   72
Problem clients
   contracts   68
   dealing with   72
   problems with   63
   saying "no"   68
Projected income   11
Proofsheets   101, 104, 105
   sample   104
Prospects, selecting   9
Protecting your business   107
Public domain   140
Public image   4
Public relations services   105
Publishers Cataloging in
      Publication Data   107

Questionable practices   178
Quitting your job   5

Receivables   49
   collecting   58
Register of Copyrights   106, 149
Relationships   8
Research   4
Reynolds, Rob, and Audrey
      Arntzen,   89
Rights   109
   All   109
   First North American Serial
      Rights   109

First Serial Rights   109
   Foreign   109
   One-time   109
   Second Serial   109
   Subsidiary   109
   Syndication   109
Riviera, Daniel J.   117

Sanford, Bruce W.   116
Scarano, Jane   22, 25, 28
Schillinger. Peggy   160
Second Serial Rights   109
Self-publishers   105
Service bureaus, choosing   161
Service clubs   20
Setting fees   40
   mistakes   40
   undercutting competition   42
Sign-off sheet, sample   103
Small businesses
   accounting   3
   economic role   3
   home-based   3
   starting out   3
   statistics   3
   survey of issues   13
   undercapitalization   4
Small claims court   11, 61
Software considerations   157
Statement of business purpose   70
Stovall, Dennis & Linny   35, 41, 67, 90, 160
Subcontractors   87, 96
Subsidiary Rights   109
Syndication Rights   109

Targeted mailings   9
Tax breaks   174
Taxes   7, 111
   deductions   178
   impact of business sale   112
   loopholes   176
   penalties   176
   recordkeeping   111
Telemarketing   22, 38
Telephone marketing   22
Temporary services   97

Terms of payment   50, 78
Time and expense software   47
   selecting   48
Time loan   81
Time management   45
Tinkel, Kathleen   29, 91, 159
Trade practices   101
Trade references   80
Trade secrets   180
Trading   61
Typesetting versus DTP   161

U.S. copyright law revision of
      1978   135
U.S. Postal Service   2
Undercapitalization   4
Underground economy   179
Unethical jobs   67
Universal Copyright
      Convention   138
Unrealistic client expectations   64

Vendors
   credit problems with   177
   trade practices   101
Village Edit, The   42
Volunteer work   25, 72

Waldmann, Heidi   15, 21, 22, 43,
      58, 160
White, Andy   163
White space   88
Wilf, Frederic M.   135
Wodaski, Ron   65, 159
Word-of-mouth marketing   19
"Work for hire"   136
Working alone   98
Working from home   6
Working on a handshake   100
Writer's Bloc   34
Writer's Market   24
*Writer's NW*   27
Written agreements. *See* Contracts
Written contracts   68, 101
Wunderlich, Judi   29

Yellow Pages
   advertising in   23
   as prospect list   29

# COLOPHON

*D*esktop Publishing: Dollars & Sense was designed by Dennis Stovall of Blue Heron Publishing. The face used for the text is Sabon set 11/14. Sabon is also used in the folios, the running heads, and the chapter numbers and titles. All subtitles are set in Univers 55. Initial drop caps of 28 points depth are used only on the unindented first paragraph of each chapter or section. Text is set on a 24 pica line, 36 lines deep.

Since this is a book on the business of "desktop" publishing, better referred to as electronic prepress services, readers may be interested in the range of tools used in its design and production.

At the time of this publication, Blue Heron Publishing, Inc., employed a network of Macintosh computers, including 2 "tricked out" Pluses, 1 Mac II with 8 megs of RAM and an E-Machines 15 inch b&w monitor, and 2 Macintosh IIcx's with 8 megs of RAM and 1 RasterOps 19 inch grayscale monitor and 1 Radius 21 inch grayscale monitor. Hard disks distributed across the network provided 550 megs of on-line storage. A DaynaFile drive with 360K, 5.25 inch and 1.44M. 3.5 inch floppy drives was used in conjunction with Software Bridge for the transfer and translation of text originating on a PC. Most of the work on this book was done on one of the IIcx's.

Once the author's text was input to our system and translated from WordPerfect for the PC, it was massaged with several tools. For text requiring considerable cleaning, batch processing, or complex parsing, Nisus was used initially. Microsoft Word was used for final editing and for rough composition because of the clean relationship between it's paragraph styles and those in Aldus PageMaker, the page layout software used. Graphics were handled either traditionally or were scanned with a Hewlett Packard ScanJet Plus. Adobe Illustrator was used for original art and graphic effects. Proofs were drawn from a LaserWriter IINT, with high resolution output rendered at a service bureau.

Many desktop publishers and others interviewed for this book asked for a *Resource List for Desktop Publishers.* So that this list can be made more responsive to the ever-changing needs of DTPers, it is available on disk or in booklet format from the author. Included is information about desktop publishing magazines, sources of clip art, desktop publishing software, other reference books, and more. To order, simply photocopy the coupon below and return to Writer's Bloc with payment.

## RESOURCE LIST FOR DESKTOP PUBLISHERS

- Magazines for the DTP industry
- Sources of clip art
- Resources for graphic artists
- And more

- Other books about DTP
- DTP software
- Resources for writers

ORDER FROM:

Writer's Bloc
1225 E. Sunset Dr. Ste. 353
Bellingham, WA 98226-3529
206/676-2415

Name _____

Title _____

Company _____

Address _____

City _____ State _____ Zip Code _____

Phone: _____
(Please include in case we have questions about your order)

☐ $7.95 booklet *or* ☐ $9.95 diskette (specify Mac or PC) plus $2 shipping for each item ordered
(if not satisfied, return within 15 days for full refund)
☐ Check or money order enclosed

*Ask about our desktop publishing business seminars*